# SPAIN

## An Illustrated History

FRED JAMES HILL

HIPPOCRENE BOOKS, INC.
NEW YORK

Typeset & designed by Fred Hill & Nick Awde /Desert♥Hearts

ISBN 0-7818-0836-7

For information, address:
HIPPOCRENE BOOKS, INC.
171 Madison Avenue
New York, NY 10016

Printed in the United States of America.

# CONTENTS

INTRODUCTION                                                                5

## THE EARLY COLONIZERS
The Phoenician and Greek Colonizers                                        15
The Iberians, Celts, and Celtiberians                                      15
The Roman Conquest                                                         16
The Roman Empire                                                           17
The Fall of the Roman Empire                                               21
The Kingdom of the Visigoths                                               23

## ISLAMIC SPAIN
The Islamic Invasion                                                       27
The Rise of Al-Andalus                                                     27
The Independent Umayyad Emirate                                            30
The Caliphate of Córdoba                                                   31
The Christian Territories and the Origins of the Reconquest                36
The Reign of Al-Mansur                                                     38
The Fall of the Caliphate of Córdoba                                       40
The *Taifas*                                                               41

## THE RECONQUEST OF SPAIN
Fernando I and the Union of Castilla-León                                  45
Alfonso VI                                                                 46
The Legend of *El Cid*                                                     46
Territorial Expansion of Castilla and Aragón                               48
The Dark Years of the 14th Century                                         50
The Nobility, Townsfolk, and Peasants                                      54

## THE GOLDEN AGE OF SPAIN
Isabella and Fernando—The Catholic Monarchs                                57
The Conquest of Granada                                                    60
The Spanish Inquisition and the Expulsion of the Jews                      62
The Colonization of the New World                                          68
Carlos I of Spain and the Hapsburgs                                        71
St. Teresa of Ávila and St. John of the Cross                              74
Felipe II                                                                  76
El Greco—Master Painter of Toledo                                          81
Felipe III                                                                 82
Cervantes and Don Quixote                                                  84
Felipe IV                                                                  85
Velázquez                                                                  87

# SPAIN UNDER THE BOURBONS

The War of the Spanish Succession                                    89
Felipe V—the Reluctant King                                          90
Fernando VI and Carlos III                                           91
Carlos IV                                                            94
The Napoleonic Wars                                                  96
The War of Independence                                              98
Spanish Liberalism and the 1812 Constitution                       100
The Restoration of the Bourbon Monarchy                             102
The Independence of Latin America                                   103
The Return of the Liberals                                          105
The Carlist Wars                                                    107
Isabel II                                                           109
Six Revolutionary Years                                             112
Benito Pérez Galdós—A Chronicler of His Time                       114
Cánovas and the System of Alternating Governments                  115
The Loss of Cuba                                                   118
Gaudí—A Towering Architectural Genius                              120
Alfonso XIII—A Reign of Crisis                                     123
The Growth of the Unions                                           125
The Disintegration of Law and Order                               127

# DICTATORSHIP AND DEMOCRACY IN THE 20TH CENTURY

The Dictatorship of Primo de Rivera                                129
The Exile of the King                                              130
The Second Spanish Republic and the Republican-Socialist Reforms   131
The Two Black Years                                                135
Militancy and the Rejection of Parliamentary Means                 137
The Military Solution                                              138
The Spanish Civil War                                              140
García Lorca and the Soul of the Gypsy                             146
Two Giants of the World of Art—Picasso and Dalí                    148
Franco's Dictatorship, the Early Years                             151
Isolation and the Failed Economics of Self-Sufficiency             153
Spain's Emergence from Isolation                                   154
The Economic Miracle                                               155
Basque Nationalism and ETA                                         158
ETA and the Rise of Violence                                       159
The Last Days of the Dictator                                      160
A Remarkable Transition to Democracy                               162
Spain under Felipe González and the Socialists                     166
Spain in the 21st Century                                          168

*INDEX*                                                            170

# INTRODUCTION

## A Nation of Change

Spain is a vibrant and fascinating country rich in culture and tradition on the one hand and, on the other, as modern and forward-looking as any of its European neighbors. Its geographical location and distinctive character make it a magnet for travelers from around the world. Every year millions of visitors pour into the country to enjoy the sights, relax on the sunny beaches of the Mediterranean Sea, and soak up the atmosphere of the fiestas—those typically Spanish regional celebrations, famed for their vitality, which can last up to two weeks and can involve anything from rather somber night-long religious processions to crowds hurling tomatoes at each other in spectacular food fights.

Looking at Spain today, it is sometimes easy to overlook the astonishing changes that have taken place in the last few decades. During the mid-1970s, as democratic European countries established ever closer economic and political links with each other, Spain still languished in isolation under the weight of a military dictatorship, headed by Francisco Franco, a general who had successfully clung to power since the end of the traumatic 1936-39 Civil War. Two successive generations had grown up knowing no other form of government.

With the passing of the old dictator in 1975, few could have foreseen the enormous transformation of the next few years, as the whole political edifice was dismantled and replaced by a Western democratic system. We often take democracy for granted in countries such as the United States, where those who fought for its introduction are somewhat mythical figures of a distant past. However, in Spain, the present constitution is so young that many of those who established it are still alive and actively involved in politics. Moreover, there was no

Spain and the Iberian Peninsula.

guarantee that they would succeed. There were moments when it seemed that a return to military rule was imminent. In 1981, Spain found itself in the grip of a dramatic struggle between the forces of democracy and authoritarianism. This battle was clear for all to see in February of that year, when a senior officer of the Civil Guard marched into the Spanish Congress, firing shots in the air, and held the president and newly-elected prime minister at gunpoint—along with every other key Spanish politician of the day. The nation watched with bated breath as the drama unfolded live on national television, the future of the country seemingly teetering on a knife-edge.

However, it soon became apparent that the conservative military forces who dreamed of a return to the days of Franco had miscalculated the change in the political and social climate, and that the old militaristic ways would no longer be tolerated. The attempted coup ended in failure, decisively breaking a long-standing tradition on the part of the army of actively intervening in politics.

Fortunately, the days of dictatorship have been laid to rest. Modern-day Spain is a democratic state that plays a full role as a member of the European Union. It is a constitutional monarchy with two elected parliamentary chambers, the Senate and Congress, and a government that is led by the prime minister. The head of state, whose powers are more symbolic than real, has been until the present King Juan Carlos— a man whose role in the transition to democracy has, as we shall see, earned him the respect of the Spanish people.

Although governed centrally from the capital of Madrid, Spain is divided into 17 autonomous regions, each of which has its own special elected assembly. This is a reflection of the various cultures that have existed in the region for centuries and that still continue to shape the lives of the 39 million-strong population, many of whom speak not just Spanish but also the official regional languages of Catalán, Basque (known as *Euskera*) and Galician (*Gallego*). The relationship between the regions has often been stormy, and indeed, in the case of the Basques, it has resulted in bloodshed. ETA, the terrorist organization calling for an independent Basque country, has been responsible for a long and violent campaign against the central Spanish government. Yet, despite tensions and a tendency for regions to guard their newly found freedom jealously, cultural diversity is, generally speaking, a cause for celebration and pride in Spain.

## A History of Conquest

The internal strife in Spain during the 20th century reflects an enormous struggle to come to terms with its past and find a place in the modern world. Spain was once the largest empire in its day, stretching across the Europe and the Americas, and reaching as far as the Philippines, bringing its own language, Catholic religion, culture, and architecture with it. Indeed, no Latin American country, nor indeed the United States, can appreciate its own past without some knowledge of Spanish history. Up until the beginning of the 19th century, Spanish territory extended across the southern part of what is today the United States and included California, Texas, and Florida.

Spain finally had to accept the fact that it was no longer a world

King Juan Carlos I of Spain.

power in 1898 when it lost Cuba, its last Latin American colony (and, significantly, its first), after a disastrous defeat at the hands of the United States Navy. But of course Spanish influence has lived on in the Americas, not least through the language, which is now the third most spoken in the world after Mandarin Chinese and English. In the United States itself, it has been estimated that more than 17 million people speak Spanish in their homes.

Plaza de España of Madrid, capital of Spain.

If Spain has been a major influence in the Americas, it in turn has been profoundly influenced by other civilizations. Once a part of the Roman Empire, it was later conquered by the Visigoths only to be invaded by Arabs and Islamic Berbers from nearby North Africa. (It is easy to overlook just how close Spain is to the African continent. Yet, there can be few experiences as exhilarating as glimpsing the North African coast across the shimmering Strait of Gibraltar from Europe's southernmost town, Tarifa. At its narrowest, the Strait is less than nine miles wide. The shortest sea crossing time between the two continents by hydrofoil is a swift 40 minutes.) For centuries Islamic civilization flourished in Spain and continued to

Roman Aqueduct of Segovia.

do so until the fall of the last Islamic kingdom of Granada in 1492, when the Iberian Peninsula was finally reconquered by the Christians.

Visitors to Spain can still see many examples of its Islamic past, exemplified by the intricate Islamic architecture of the Mosque of Córdoba or the Alhambra in Granada. Interestingly, across the sea in

Plaque on the government building in Málaga acknowledging its varied history as a Phoenician trading post, Carthaginian emporium, and subsequent dominion of the Romans, Visigoths, and Byzantines. It continues: "It was a port under the domination of the Muslims, lying between the Mediterranean and the Atlantic, between Europe and Africa. It was conquered by the Catholic Monarchs in August 1487."

Outer wall of the Great Mosque of Córdoba, founded in the 8th century.

Morocco, the town of Chechaouen owes its Spanish-Andalusian appearance to the fact that it was built by Spanish Muslims exiled from Spain in the 15th century. It is also fascinating to note that many names of Spanish towns and places are derived from Arabic, as are many words in the Spanish language. The name Andalucía itself is derived from the Arabic *Al-Andalus*, meaning "The Isle of the Vandals."

Conquest, therefore, is the key theme that runs through much of Span's complex and volatile history. In the same year that the Christians defeated the last Muslim stronghold, Christopher Columbus, sponsored by the Spanish Crown, chanced upon the Americas. It opened up a whole new continent for the Spanish Conquistadors, steeped in the tradition and culture forged by centuries of war against the Muslims, to conquer. Their lives and adventures became the stuff of myths and legends that filtered into the national consciousness. It is notable that in the 20th century, General Franco, who made his military career in campaigns in North Africa, drew on the myths of the reconquest of Spain by referring to his fight against those who defended the Republic in the 1930s as a "Christian Crusade" to save Spain from the evils of Communism and atheism.

## A Land of Mountains and Differing Climes

There is a saying in Spain, *"la geografía manda"* ("geography has the last word"), and certainly the country's physical characteristics and climate are worth bearing in mind when it comes to its history. Spain, which is roughly twice the size of Oregon, also shares the Iberian Peninsula with Portugal. It further includes the Balearic Islands in the Mediterranean Sea, the Canary Islands off the west coast of Africa, and the enclave towns of Ceuta and Melilla, which lie on the North Moroccan coast.

Although incredibly green and wet in the north and northwest with mild temperatures, the Mediterranean coast and the south receive little rainfall and temperatures average around 10°C in winter, seldom falling below 5°C, and during the long hot dry summers often reach well over

35°C. The center of Spain is a vast elevated plateau that occupies more than half of the country, and here the winters are long and cold followed by blisteringly hot summers.

In addition to its varied climate, Spain is remarkable for its mountains. The Iberian Peninsula is one of the most mountainous areas in Europe. To the north the Pyrenees cut the peninsula off from the rest of Europe, and throughout the country there are various ranges—the highest being in the Sierra Nevada in the south, which reaches over 10,000 feet. From the earliest times, the mountainous terrain has had a major influence on Spanish history, since it made crossing the country difficult, hemming in the various cultures that flourished in the region and making it a supremely difficult task for invading forces to impose their authority over them. And with an abundance of minerals, extensive coasts to fish, and regions suited to the cultivation of olives and grapes, the land held many attractions for would-be colonizers.

Ruins of an Iron Age *castro* in Coaña, Asturias. *Castros* were fortified settlements characterized by their circular houses, paved streets, and exterior walls.

# THE EARLY COLONIZERS

## The Phoenician and Greek Colonizers

Spain began to make its mark on written history with the arrival of adventurous settlers from civilizations that were based far away in the eastern Mediterranean. The eastern and southern regions of the Iberian Peninsula became part of a complex trading system that continually brought different cultures into contact with each other. Some of the earlier colonizers were the Phoenicians, who arrived on the shores of the peninsula around two thousand years ago and established the city of Gadir, today the Spanish port of Cádiz. The new colonizers were a seafaring people whose country, Phoenicia, lay around the coastal region now occupied by Lebanon and Israel. They were lured to the Iberian Peninsula by the rich deposits of metals such as silver, copper, and tin. New colonies such as Malaca (today known as Málaga) sprang up in the area of Andalucia. With colonies throughout the Mediterranean, they came to dominate trade in the region. After the defeat of Phoenicia by the Assyrians, the Phoenicians transferred their power base to North African city of Carthage, situated in present-day Tunisia.

Around 600BC, Greek traders began to arrive on the shores of the peninsula in search of minerals and eventually established permanent settlements along the Mediterranean coast. They brought with them their art, such as music and sculpture, and left a lasting mark on the peoples with whom they came into contact. With the arrival of the Greeks and the Phoenicians also came the introduction of new technologies in iron-work, along with the potter's wheel.

## The Iberians, Celts, and Celtiberians

It was the Greeks who first began to refer to the inhabitants of the region as Iberians, and thus the land as Iberia. The Iberians were not a unified people but a mixture of different tribes that lived along the Mediterranean coast of Spain. They lived in walled hilltop towns and, amongst other activities, engaged in agricultural and livestock farming. They were keen sculptors, producing small well-crafted bronze and ceramic figures as religious offerings, as well as large stone sculptures depicting humans and animals. The north of the peninsula was settled

by Celts who first arrived around 1000BC from Central Europe and France. These too were a mixture of different tribes, one of which was the Galaicos who lived in what is today known as Galicia, in the north-west of Spain. They built *castros*, which were fortified settlements with paved streets and circular houses—many examples of which can still be seen today. In the center of the peninsula were the highly war-like Celtiberians who, as their name suggests, developed a culture that was greatly influenced by both their neighbors, the Celts and Iberians. It was not until the arrival of the Romans that the various peoples living in the peninsula would be brought together under a single political entity.

The mysterious Lady of Elche, an Iberian stone sculpture, believed to date from the 4th century BC. She may have been a goddess or an Iberian princess.

## The Roman Conquest

In the third century BC, Rome and Carthage—the city founded by the Phoenicians—engaged in a long power struggle against each other to dominate the western Mediterranean. After losing the First Punic War (264-241 BC) to Rome, the Carthaginians lost their influence over the Mediterranean islands of Sicily, Corsica, and Sardinia. Carthage subsequently attempted to make up for its losses by strengthening its position in the Iberian Peninsula. Despite atttempts to reach a settlement in the region, the rivalry between the two powers erupted into open conflict after the great Carthaginian general, Hannibal, attacked the strategic city-state of Sagunto in 219BC. The city, near present-day Valencia on the east coast of Spain, promptly called on the help of its Roman allies for help. This ignited a second major war between the powers, resulting in the defeat of the Carthaginians, who were finally forced to flee the peninsula in 206BC. Spain, or *Hispaniae* as it became known to the new rulers, had now become part of the huge Roman Empire.

The Iberian Peninsula, with its wealth of minerals—especially gold and silver—and agricultural lands, was a coveted acquisition for Rome, which began in earnest to stamp its authority over the region. However, it was to be a lengthy and turbulent process.

Romanization meant imposing the social, economic, and political structures of the Roman Empire onto a country inhabited by a mixture of peoples whose cultures and level of social development varied greatly. The first wave of pacification in the eastern and southern Mediterranean region of the peninsula presented less of a problem. This area contained the more developed urban areas which had a history of colonization and were more receptive to the new changes. Yet the further the Romans moved towards the less developed areas in the center and north of the peninsula, the more difficult it became. Here they found tremendous opposition from fierce tribes, who stubbornly refused to surrender their traditional ways of life. It took two hundred years before the Romans eventually brought the last remaining regions—Cantabria and Asturias in the far north—under their control, and thus completed their conquest of the peninsula.

## The Roman Empire

As the Romans pacified new territories, they established a network of new cities, connected by major roads, which became the administrative centers for the surrounding regions. Many cities and towns in present-

Remains of a Roman temple, Córdoba.

day Spain trace their origins to Roman times, such as Mérida (Emerita Augusta), León (Legio), Barcelona (Barcino), and Tarragona (Tarraco).

Throughout Spain the native inhabitants adopted Roman customs and laws. A highly significant development was the adoption of the Latin language, which was used throughout Spain and gradually led to the abandonment of indigenous tongues. Different from that found in Roman texts, the Latin of Spain was a vulgar brand, which was spread by Roman soldiers. Today, modern Spanish, like the other Romance languages of Europe, such as French and Italian, can trace its roots directly back to this language of empire.

Detail of a first-century Roman mosaic, Córdoba.

Education and the arts were also areas that developed under the influence of the Romans. Spain would prove to be no mere backwater, but would eventually produce its fair share of renowned Romans, such as the rhetorician Quintilian; the poets Lucan and Martial; the philosopher Seneca; and the second-century emperors, Hadrian and Trajan.

Spain soon became the most important economic province in the Roman Empire. Like the Phoenicians before them, the Romans were principally interested in metals. Spanish mines worked by slaves produced huge quantities of metal for export to Rome. The most important mines, especially those producing the gold and silver used to create money, were jealously guarded by the state. Apart from its mineral exports, Spain was also major supplier of grain and other agricultural products to Rome, such as olive oil and wine. Similarly there was a thriving textile industry, producing materials in wool and flax, which competed with the Mediterranean market. Another favorite export was garum, a tangy sauce made from fish.

With the Romans, of course, came their impressive architectural skills: aqueducts to bring water into towns, bridges, ampitheaters, temples and public baths. The imposing aqueduct in Segovia is just one of many outstanding examples of Roman architecure that can still be seen today.

The Romans introduced their own gods into Spain, such as Jupiter and Minerva. Since no attempt was made to eradicate local beliefs, many of these existed side by side with those of the Romans. With time the Roman gods were assimilated by the indigenous population, either replacing their own or creating a fusion of the two.

Christianity was different altogether. The Romans were keen to stop the spread of what was for them a highly subversive new religion, and pursued a policy of ruthless suppression. Although the exact date of the arrival of Christianity into Spain is not known, certainly by the middle

Ruins of a Roman ampitheater, Málaga.

The Roman aqueduct of Segovia was built in the first century AD and continued to be used as late as the 1940s.

of the 3rd century AD it had caught a firm hold. Like other parts of the empire, Spain had its share of Christian martyrs who suffered cruel deaths at the hands of the Roman authories for their faith.

In the early 14th century, however, their fortunes turned with the Roman Emperor Constantine's conversion to Christianity. At the end of the century, Christianity became the official state religion and subsequently flourished.

## The Fall of the Roman Empire

Spain thrived under the Romans, enjoying a long period of stability and wealth. However, as part of the Roman Empire, its fate was inextricably linked with the fortunes of Rome. In the 3rd century AD, disaster

The Roman Bridge of Córdoba—later rebuilt by the Muslims.

began to loom. The empire's frontiers came under increasing attacks from various barbarian tribes, and it began to suffer severe internal social and political strife. Rome went into steady decline. By the end of the fourth century, it had split into two separate empires, east and west, with Rome and Constantinople as their capitals. After its last emperor was deposed in 476, the Western Roman Empire finally fell, overrun by successive waves of barbarians.

Several decades before the curtain fell on Rome, Spain had descended into lawlessness. In 409AD, three different ferocious Germanic tribes—the Vandals, Suebi, and Alans—came swarming over the Pyrenees, bringing chaos and devastation as they pillaged and ravaged the country. In an attempt to rid the peninsula of them, the Romans enlisted the support of another equally warlike Germanic tribe, the Visigoths, to fight as mercenaries. They were successful in driving out the Vandals and Alans, although they failed to dislodge the Suebi who held fast in the northwestern region of Galicia.

In return for their help, the Romans allowed the Visigoths, who were once again on the move, to establish their new headquarters in southern France. In 455, their services were called on once again to put an end to Suebian expansion into neighboring regions of Galicia. In the conflict that ensued, the Visigoths were able to drive the Suebi back into their original corner. Having spent a great deal of time fighting the Romans' battles in Spain, the Visigoths not surprisingly established a strong presence in the peninsula; and when the Western Roman Empire fianally collapsed, they became the new lords of the land.

# The Kingdom of the Visigoths

The Visigoths ruled over Spain for two centuries, establishing a kingdom that comprised most of the Iberian Peninsula, and had as its capital the city of Toledo in the center of the country. The kingdom initially included extensive territory in France but, with the exception of a small strip of territory in south, it was lost after the Franks defeated them at the Battle of Vouille in 507AD.

The Visigoths were descendents of the Goths, a warlike Germanic people believed to have originated in Scandinavia. After migrating into central Europe, the Visigoths went their own separate way and eventually arrived in Roman-controlled territory. As we have seen, their Gothic fierceness was put to good use by the Romans, who used their military services in exchange for lands on which to settle. The Visigoths certainly confirmed their reputation for fierceness during their rule over Spain—a time in which their ruling classes were riddled by internecine strife and successive kings were overthrown.

The 200,000 new Visigothic invaders were far less numerous than the three to four million Hispano-Romans that they conquered. Little is known about the relationship between the Visigoths and their new subjects, yet it is clear that there was a steady overall decline in the fortunes of Spain, which had thrived under the Romans.

The real challenge to Visigoth rule came not from the more sophisticated and Romanized sections of the population, but from the Suebi and traditionally unruly mountain peoples in the north—in particular the Basques and Cantabrians. Also, to the south, the

Byzantines of the Eastern Roman Empire held substantial territories including Málaga and Cartagena. It was not until the second half of the 6th century, during the reign of King Leovigild, that the Visigoths managed to get a firm grip over the peninsula and bring about a semblance of unity.

A major source of tension between the new rulers and the native population was religion. The Visigoths practised a variant form of Christianity, known as Arianism; whereas the Hispano-Roman population was Catholic. It was not until the conversion of Leovigild's son, King Reccared, towards the end of the 6th century that the matter was resolved with the imposition of Catholicism as the official religion of the Visigothic kingdom. This opened the door for the Catholic hierarchy of clergymen that had survived from the Roman days to participate in and play a major role in the running of the state through councils headed by the king. For Jews living in the region, it was a different story altogether. Vicious campaigns were unleashed forcing them to convert to Christianity or face the confiscation of their possessions, the imposttition of punitive taxes, and even slavery. It was not until the arrival of the Muslims that their life would once again improve, and Judaism would be free to flourish in the peninsula.

The nobility and clergy became extremely poweful during the reign of the Visigoths. After the conflicts and wars that had plagued the peninsula, many of the small proprietors lost their lands—only those who had armies to protect themselves managed to hold on to their possessions, and this included the most powerful factions of the aristocracy and clergy. Furthermore, the two groups fought tooth and nail to keep their lands free from interference by the monarchy; and, given enough provocation, they were quite likely turn their private armies against the central government.

Successive kings attempted to curb the power of the nobles and bishops, but with little success. Beginning in the 7th century, the noblemen became so powerful that they were able to elect their own monarchs—a development that heightened the kingdom's instability as incessant disputes erupted over who would succeed to the throne. In the latter part of the 7th century, one Visigothic king by the name of Wamba fell foul of the nobility by attempting to impose military obligations on it. He was promptly deposed and the noblemen saw to it that future monarchs refrained from unwelcome displays of regal authority.

The reign of the Visigoths also coincided with rise of feudalism that held sway throughout the European world of the Middle Ages. Life in Spain for the commoner could thus be extremely harsh, especially for those not fortunate to be born into free families. These were the serfs, who had no rights and were victims of the summary justice of their masters. They could be bought and sold and were doomed to a slave-like existence, working the huge estates to which they were bonded. It was this pattern that was to take firm root and dominate the countryside in Christian Spain for centuries to come.

Until its final days, the Visigothic kingdom continued to be plagued by confrontations between the monarchy and the dissastified nobility. When Rodrigo was crowned the last Visigothic king in 710, he, like his predecessors, found himself the ruler of a highly unstable kingdom. In addition to immediately contending with a civil war that had broken out over his leadership, Rodrigo was forced to launch a military campaign against insurrectionist mountain tribes in the north. The collapse of the Visigothic Kingdom was not far off, and when it came it would be swift.

The Iberian Peninsula under the rule of the Muslims in the 8th century.

# ISLAMIC SPAIN

## The Islamic Invasion

In the early summer of 711, an Arab-led Berber army crossed from North Morocco to the southernmost point of Spain, landing on a huge rock that juts out majestically from the mainland into the sea. The Arabs named the rock *Jebel Tariq* ("Rock of Tariq"), from which modern-day Gibraltar derives its name, in honor of the general who led the expedition. It was a momentous event that marked the beginning of centuries of Islamic rule in Spain. General Tariq ibn Ziyad's expedition was the latest in a campaign of territorial expansion by the Arab Empire, which had recently conquered North Africa.

Although an Arab himself, Tariq's army was made up of Berbers, a people who had for centuries inhabited North Africa. During the 7th century, after the Arabs invaded and conquered their territory, many Berbers adopted the Islamic faith of their new rulers. Tariq and his Berbers marched to Guadelete, some sixteen miles east of Cádiz, where they confronted King Rodrigo's army. The Visigoths were no match for the Islamic invaders and in the battle that followed in July 711, Rodrigo was soundly defeated, losing his throne and very probably his life, since he was never heard of again. Meeting no resistance, Tariq marched on to the Visigoth capital of Toledo. Once there, he was reinforced by an Arab army of 18,000 men led by the governor of North Africa, Musa ibn Nusayr. The invaders inflicted a devasting and decisive blow against the Visigoths. By 714, practically the entire Iberian Peninsula lay under Arab rule.

## The Rise of Al-Andalus

Spain, known to the Arabs as *Al-Andalus*, had now become part of the great Umayyad Empire. The Umayyads were an Arab dynasty, headed

Aerial view of the Rock of Gibraltar, where Tariq landed with his Berber army.

by caliphs, whose power base was in the Syrian capital of Damascus. A caliph held the highest postion of authority in the Muslim temporal world. The Umayyads were responsible for the early spread of Islam, the religion of the Prophet Muhammad who died in 632, throughout its vast empire. At its peak, the empire stretched east from the borders of China all the way across North Africa to the shores of the Atlantic Ocean. After their victory in the Iberian Peninsula, they crossed over into France and eventually reached as far as the Loire Valley, a distance of less than two hundred miles from Paris. After the Battle of Poitiers in 732, however, the Umayyads were defeated and forced to end their expansion into French territory.

The first few decades of Arab rule in Spain were turbulent. The Umayyad Caliphate faced a hard struggle in attempting to impose its authority over its newly-won territories and in curbing the anarchic behavior of the independently-minded Arab and Berber armies. Then events took a dramatic new turn. In 750, as a result of political upheavals in Damascus, the Umayyads were overthrown and replaced by a new dynasty called the Abbasids, who ruled from their capital of

Baghdad. With their home country in turmoil, the Spanish Umayyads established independent rule in Spain—first as an emirate between 756 and 929, and then as a caliphate from 929 until 1031.

Fortunately for the Christian and Jewish communities in the peninsula, their respective members were considered to be fellow "Peoples of the Book (Old Testament)" under Islamic law. This recognition permitted the practice of Christianity and Judaism, upon payment of special taxes. Although these religions lost the majority of their followers to Islam—no doubt an influence of the extra tax burden—they still commanded a great many belivers. Those who retained their Christian faith became know as *mozárabes*, a term that reflected their gradual fostering of certain Arabic traits, such as dress and the adoption of the Arabic language. Many Jews, who had fled Spain to escape the terrible persecution of the Visigoths, took advantage of the new laws and returned. With Muslims, Jews, and Christians all

The Arabs who spearheaded the Islamic Berber invasion of the Iberian Peninsula, while remaining true to their desert origins, also brought with them the Mediterranean culture and learning that Europe had lost in the Dark Ages.

Berber peasants—the Berbers were one of the diverse Islamic groups who collectively became known as Moors and settled in the Iberian Peninsula.

living side by side, customs and traditions overlapped and Spain became a veritable melting pot. Furthermore, intermarriages between Berbers, Arabs, and Europeans saw to it that physical characteristics similarly intermingled throughout the peninsula. In Spanish history the term *moro*, or Moor, has been used as blanket term covering what in fact was a diverse mixture of peoples including Arabians, Yemenites, Syrians, and Berbers— all who had united under the banner of Islam.

## The Independent Umayyad Emirate

The first emir of the independent Emirate of Al-Andalus was Abd al-Rahman, who established his capital in Córdoba. He was the sole survivor of the Umayyad dynasty, which had been massacred at the murderous hands of the Abbasids. Abd al-Rahman was followed by a succession of emirs whose rule was beset by ongoing political crises as they attempted to maintain centralized control over Al-Andalus. One serious problem lay in the very north of the Iberian Peninsula, in the frontier lands between the emirate and Christian-held territories. On the Arab side, these territories were left in the hands of rebellious chiefs who, with their own small armies, governed them as if they were their own miniature kingdoms, free to make their own deals and treaties with their Christian neighbors. To keep control and prevent them from becoming fully-fledged independent kingdoms, the Umayyad emirs came to rely on a large mercenary army to impose their central authority. Maintaining troops was a costly business and required exacting higher taxes. This situation created a great deal of resentment, which in turn led to serious confrontations between the government and the population in the capital. Yet, despite the troubles, there were intermittent periods of peace and stability, such as the one that allowed for work to begin on the construction of the spectacular Mosque of Córdoba in 785. Furthermore, under the patronage of Emir Abd al-Rahman II from 822 to 853, the arts and sciences began to blossom, laying the foundations for the glorious age of the Caliphate of Córdoba.

## The Caliphate of Córdoba

The man who managed to impose central rule and bring an end to the frequent rebellions and internal disorder was Emir Abd al-Rahman III, who came to power in 912. In 926, he assumed the all-powerful role of caliph, ushering in a new era of Muslim rule. Under Abd al-Rahman III and his three successors, the Islamic Caliphate of Córdoba reigned supreme in the Iberian Peninsula; and even the Christian territories in the north were forced to recognize its authority and pay tribute.

Abd al-Rahman III was a fine example of the mixed identity that was being forged out of the various cultures and peoples of the peninsula. His mother was a Christian concubine, most probably from the Basque region. His grandfather was the son of an Arab Cordovan emir, and his grandmother was a Christian princess who had been sent by her father, the king of Navarra in the north, as an offering to cement close ties with Al-Andalus. By all accounts, Abd al-Rahman III was

Part of the forest of 850 red and white pillars that fill the interior of the Mosque of Córdoba, begun under Abd al-Rahman I in 785AD.

One of the many doors to the Mosque of Córdoba, a fine example of
Moorish craftsmanship.

Arab watermill, on the River Guadalquivir, Córdoba, which was used
to irrigate the surrounding area.

light-skinned, blue-eyed and had reddish hair—it was even said that he dyed it in order to appear more Arabic. He spoke fluent Arabic as well as the Latin-based language used by the Christians.

The city of Córdoba that he and his successors ruled over was truly spectacular. At its peak, with an estimated population of 100,000, it was the largest city in Muslim Spain and was famous throughout the Arab world for its large markets, clean streets, baths, and mosques. The city gained an outstanding reputation for learning and scholarship. The study of the arts and sciences flourished and included astronomy, medicine, and mathematics. It was through the Spanish Muslims that the concept of zero, decimalization, and written Arab numerical figures (upon which those in the West are based, replacing the cumbersome Roman numerals) were introduced into Europe. Under the patronage of the caliphs, especially during the reign of Al-Hakem II between 961 and 976, Córdoba boasted one the greatest libraries in the Islamic world and one without rival in Europe. In fact its reputation was such that it attracted not only scholars from the Arab world but Christians from around Europe. The city also had a thriving Jewish population, by whose merit Córdoba became a major center for Hebrew scholarship.

New industries also thrived in Mulsim Córdoba, which boasted glassware and pottery of exceptional quality. Similarly, highly skilled silk weavers and carpet makers ensured that their excellent products became famed throughout the Iberian Peninsula. With Islam came a new approach to the visual arts that was quite distinct from that of the Christians. In Islam, the ultimate purpose of art was to strengthen the faith of believers by using beauty to remind them of the transcendent nature of God.

Therefore, rather than concentrating on natural images of humans and animals, the Muslims favored abstract designs such as the exquisite geometrical and plant patterns to be found in their calligraphy, woodwork, textiles, ceramics and in the stonecarvings and mosaics that adorned their architecture. However, Moorish art was far from purist, and as the various styles used to adorn the Great Mosque of Córdoba

Examples of intricate Islamic stonecarvings and mosaics featuring geometrical and floral designs. The second picture includes a magnification of the pattern (inset).

testify, Spanish Muslims drew on a whole array of influences, which ranged from Roman and Carthaginian pillars to Visigothic floral designs.

# The Christian Territories and the Origins of the Reconquest

After the Muslim conquest, the Visigothic Kings had taken a beating but were by no means finished. The onslaught of the Muslim invasion had sent the Visigoths running to the protection of the Cantabrian mountain range to the far north of the Iberian Peninsula, in the region of Asturias. It was here at the Battle of Covadonga in 722 that the Christians had their first significant military success against the Muslims. This symbolic event is looked upon in Spanish history as the beginning of the *Reconquista*—the reconquest of the Iberian Peninsula from the Muslims. If this was indeed the beginning, then it was to take another 770 years for the process to be completed, with the fall of the last Muslim kingdom of Granada in 1492.

9th-century Church of San Miguel de Lillo, near Oviedo in Asturias, a region that was the center of Christian resistance to the Muslims and the nucleus of the reconquest.

Covadonga has become as legendary as the life of the man who led the battle, known to history as simply "Pelayo." Mystery surrounds the life of this Asturian Visigoth warrior, who became king of Asturias and died around 737. Pelayo, who may have been related to King Rodrigo, managed to escape the onslaught of the Muslims at the Battle of Guadelete, and took refuge in Asturias with other fleeing Visigoths. He subsequently led uprisings against the Muslims and, at one point, was even seized and held as a hostage. Pelayo's tiny realm of Asturias became the nucleus of Christian expansion into Muslim territory. Over the next two centuries, the kingdom gradually pushed southwards over the mountains to León and into the valley of the River Duero, re-establishing the Christian-Muslim frontier. This new territory, together with Asturias, became known as the Kingdom of León.

The gradual occupation by Christians of the sparsely-populated lands to the east of León led to the creation of the principality of Castilla. Lying along the wild frontier, it was an extremely dangerous place to inhabit. There was a continuous threat of Muslims assaults from the south. Not for nothing did it become known as Castilla, the land of "castles." Along the frontiers, the Christian castles looked out across the plains in constant readiness to resist the attacks of the Muslims. In 946, Castilla became a kingdom in its own right and later, after its union with León, became the most powerful Christian state in the peninsula—a major driving force behind the reconquest and Spain's subsequent rise to power in the world.

## The Reign of Al-Mansur

The Christian kingdoms in the north found one of their worst enemies in Al-Mansur the powerful vizier of the Caliph Hisham II, son of the famed Caliph Al-Hakem II, who had helped Córdoba achieve such great heights. Al-Mansur was born into a family of Arab descent in Algeciras in southern Spain. A clever and ruthless politician, Al-Mansur rapidly worked his way to the top of Al-Hakem II's government to

Roof and interior of the Arab Baths of Girona, Catalonia, built in the Muslim style in 1194.

eventually become the caliph's right-hand man. From there, he went on to become a skillful military commander; his ferocious campaigns against the kingdom of León earned him the great respect of his army.

After Al-Hakem II's death in 976, Al-Mansur governed in the name of the caliph's young son, Hisham II, who was actively discouraged from taking part in the politics of the country. Al-Mansur went on to assume dictatorial powers, and relying heavily on his army of Berbers, ruthlessly quashed any opposition in the Caliphate—especially in the restless frontier lands. Without the financial means to support an ever increasing army, Al-Mansur led expeditions for booty in Spanish Christian territories in the north, including Santiago de Compostela, Barcelona, León, and Pamplona.

In the eyes of Muslims, Al-Mansur was a hero: an extremely pious man who carried out his expeditions under the banner of Islam. (On these expeditions, he carried a copy of the Qur'an written in his own hand, as well as a "death gown" in preparation for his death on the battlefield.) To the Christians, on the other hand, he was a scourge—a ruthless leader whose eventual death during a military expedition led one Christian chronicler to note that "he was seized by the Devil and buried in Hell."

# The Fall of the Caliphate of Córdoba

Al-Mansur was succeeded in office by his son Abd al-Malik, who also ruled on behalf of the politically ineffectual Hisham II. Abd al-Malik continued the aggressive policies of his father and, supported by his Berber army, delivered a devasting blow to Barcelona, followed by attacks on Castilla, León, and Aragón.

His early death in 1008, however, left the caliphate in a vulnerable position as various contenders fought for the leadership. The first to succeed him was his brother, but he was assassinated within a few months. An extraordinary battle for the caliphate followed, in which Muslim and Christian alliances were formed to definitively settle the issue—a goal that would not be achieved for some time. Muhammed II initially gained the caliphate, though the Berbers' choice for the office was a leader named Sulayman. He immediately appealed to the Castilians for military support, and they, together with Berber forces, soundly defeated Muhammed II at Córdoba. Thus deposed by Sulayman, Muhammad II himself enlisted the support of Christian forces—the Catalans, in this case. Once again the attacking Muslim-Christian army prevailed, and Muhammed II regained the caliphate. The chaotic struggle, however, did not end there. For Muhammad II was killed shortly after his reemergence, at which point the indefatigable Sulayman once more attacked Córdoba. After a siege that lasted two and a half years, he established a rule that effected little but the ruin of Córdoba.

Thereafter, a series of caliphs rapidly rose and fell. With the downfall of Hisham III in 1031, however, Ummayad rule was irrevocably extinguished. The Caliphate of Córdoba, burdened by the costs of war, disintegrated and fragmented into petty kingdoms known

Fortified walls of Gibralfaro Castle overlooking Málaga, built by the Muslims in the 14th century.

as *taifas*—a political system which was to last until the fall of the last Muslim kingdom of Granada, in 1492.

## The *Taifas*

There were no less than twenty-three *taifas* in Al-Andalus, each with its own ruler who was continually at war with the other rulers. In such a volatile world, it was up to each *taifa* to decide how best to protect itself and which allies to choose. Often this meant calling on the help of Christians who were only too happy to oblige. This state of virtual anarchy gave the Christian kingdoms, which were already exacting

The main gate of the 11th-century Alcázaba of the emirs of Málaga, who carved themselves out an independent kingdom during the era of the *taifas.*

heavy tribute from the bordering northern *taifas* in return for their independence, a perfect opportunity to sack and pillage Muslim towns. Islamic unity was thus dealt a severe blow. From this point forward the Christians had the upper hand, and the gradual process of the reconquest of the land from the Muslims began in earnest.

The Iberian Peninsula in the mid-11th century.

# THE RECONQUEST OF SPAIN

In the early 11th century, there were four Christian Kingdoms in Spain —Castilla, León, Navarra, Aragón—and the counties of Catalonia. But there was little unity between them as they fought not only the Muslims but also each other. Yet, very gradually these kingdoms were to forge alliances and unions and present a united front to the Muslims, rallying behind the banner of Christianity. By the year 1230, these had merged into the two main kingdoms of León-Castilla and Aragón-Catalonia. However, it was not until the joint reign of the Catholic Monarchs, Isabella and Fernando, that these two kingdoms would invite and finally conquer the last Muslim stronghold of Granada in 1492.

## Fernando I and the Union of Castilla-León

The 11th-century Castilian king, Fernando I, went some way to forging Christian unity by successfully, albeit temporarily, merging the kingdoms of Castilla and León in 1037. The new power created a formidable challenge to the Muslim *taifas*. Yet Fernando I was careful not to upset the status quo when it came to the Muslims. There were great profits to be made from the tributes extracted by the Muslim kingdoms of Zaragoza, Toledo, Sevilla and Badajoz, in return for which Castilla-León guaranteed protection from attacks by Christians or other Muslim *taifas*.

It was a practice that became firmly rooted in the peninsula and amounted to a protection racket on a massive scale. The Christian kings, taking advantage of the weakened and fragmented Muslim kingdoms, demanded tribute payment—principally in gold—from various leaders in return for military aid and a guarantee to leave them in peace. These payments, known as *parias*, became a major source of revenue for the kings. In the complex politics of the time, it became the norm for Christians to make (and break) alliances with Muslims against other Muslims, depending on where the best rewards lay.

# Alfonso VI

If Al-Mansur had been the scourge of the Christians, Alfonso VI, during his rule as king of León-Castilla from 1072 to 1109, was likewise the bane of the Muslims. Like his father Fernando I before him, he extracted high payments from the *taifa* kingdoms, including Granada. Yet Alfonso VI had territorial designs on the non-Christian territories to the south. In 1085, he delivered a serious blow to the Muslims when he attacked Toledo. As it turned out, the city was fortunate. Since it had surrendered without a struggle, the inhabitants were spared the horrors of execution or enslavement and the terms of peace were conciliatory. Alfonso VI showed the same tolerance that the Muslims were known for, and upon payment of taxes, permitted the inhabitants of the city to continue to practice their religion, keep their possessions, and come and go as they pleased. He appointed a *mozárabe* (the name given to Arabized Christians) as governor. The loss of Toledo appalled the Muslim kings of Granada, Sevilla and Badajoz, who saw the development as the possible beginning of a wider pattern of Castillian expansion. They called on the help of the fanatical North African Muslim group, the Almoravids, who subsequently launched an aggressive religious war to restore Muslim rule in Spain. In a confrontation with the Almoravids, Alfonso VI was delivered a series of blows, yet managed to hold on to Toledo. After his death in 1108, his kingdom was divided amongst his children and a long period of civil war began, temporarily putting an end to the unity of Castilla-León.

# The Legend of *El Cid*

The reconquest of Spain is a period in Spanish history that has given rise to countless legends and tales of bravery in the war against the Muslims. One Castilian nobleman whose life inspired one of the most enduring myths in Spanish history was Rodrigo Díaz de Vivar, better known as *El Cid*, from the Arabic *Al-Sayyid* meaning "The Lord." Rodrigo had fallen out with Alfonso VI, after making the king swear in public that he had played no part in his own brother's murder, and was rewarded for his troubles by being exiled in 1081. He then embarked on a career as a daring warrior who was just as likely to attack Christian strongholds as Muslim ones. Before long he threw himself into the task of pillaging the countryside and exacting tribute from the various *taifas*, growing exceedingly rich in the

The Alcázar of Toledo. The city was a major center for the Visigoths, Muslims, and Christians alike.

process. Certainly capable of extreme ruthlessness against Muslim and Christian adversaries alike, he was rich enough to have his own private army and ended up seizing Valencia, which he ruled until his death in 1099. His legend was immortalized in the *Poem of the Cid*, the earliest and greatest surviving literary epic of Castilla, composed several decades after his death. In the process, Rodrigo the man was transformed into a hero whose exploits against the Muslims symbolized the spirit of the age.

The Palacio de la Aljafería, Zaragoza—a relic of Aragón's Moorish *taifa*, dating back to the 11th century.

## Territorial Expansion of Castilla and Aragón

The 13th century was a key period in the rise of Christian Spain. At first, the Christian expansion was checked first by the invasion of the Almoravids, and then again in 1146 by the invasion of another fundamentalist group, the Almohad Berbers, based in Morocco. However, a new powerful Christian alliance—formed by Castilla, Aragón, and Navarra—closed ranks and decisively beat the Almohad army at the Battle of Las Navas de Tolosa, in 1212. It was a major turning point for the Christian kingdoms, which now launched a major thrust into Muslim-held territories. Within forty years practically the whole of the Iberian Peninsula was under the rule of Christian kings.

Jaime I of Aragón and Fernando III of Castilla-León were the principal players in the territorial expansion of the 13th century. Under Jaime I, the *taifas* to the east suffered a major blow, beginning with the Muslim-held Balearic Islands in the Mediterranean. In 1229, Jaime I's Aragonese fleet set sail to conquer the islands, and within a few years all

A scene from a Royal Hunt in the 13th century led by King Alfonso X,
ruler of Castilla-León (1252-84). Above are displayed Spanish
household items of the period, including a wooden
pitcher and oil lamps.

of them—except Minorca, which agreed to pay tribute to Aragón in
return for its independence—were absorbed into the Aragonese kingdom.
Jaime I then turned his attention southwards to the important Muslim
city of Valencia. Having taken control of all the key towns on the way, he
then blockaded the city by sea. Valencia endured two years of siege before
finally surrendering in 1238. Five years later, Murcia was also conquered.

Meanwhile Fernando III, king of the recently reunited kingom of
Castilla-León, marched south and laid seige to Córdoba, once the city
that had been the crowning glory of Islamic civilization in Spain, but
which had now fallen into decline. It fell in 1236, and as soon as the
Great Mosque was ritually cleansed and consecrated as a cathedral,
Fernando III entered the city and heard mass. It was a landmark event
for Christian Spain, which had reclaimed a city that for so long been

the seat of Islamic authority in the Iberian Peninsula. In another highly symbolic act, the bells that had been seized by Al-Mansur in 997 and had hung in the Great Mosque of Córdoba ever since were finally returned to the Cathedral of Santiago in Galicia.

Fernando III did not stop there, but marched on to Sevilla, now the greatest city in Muslim Spain, and laid a long and grueling siege to it. After two years, conditions in the beleaguered city were utterly miserable. There was little food and water, and disease was rampant. When the city finally surrendered, all Muslims were ordered to leave the city with only the possessions they could carry. When the Christians finally entered in 1248, they found a ghost town of empty streets and houses.

After centuries of political turmoil and expansion, and with these recent landmark gains, Spain emerged with four distinct Christian kingdoms that hemmed in Granada, the last Muslim stronghold. These were Castilla, Aragón, Navarra, and the newly independent kingdom of Portugal. After incorporating León, Asturia, Galicia, and huge territorial gains in the south, Castilla was the largest of the kingdoms. It also imposed the conditions of peace upon the kingdom of Granada, which was required to pay tribute and lend military assitance when required.

## The Dark Years of the 14th Century

After the heady days of the Christian conquests, the 14th century brought with it economic decline, wars, and social unrest. Added to this was the appalling loss of life suffered at the hands of the Black Death that swept across Europe and into the Iberian Peninsula.

Nobody was safe from the dreadful plague—not even royal households, as the death of King Alfonso XI of Castilla in 1350 was to prove. The disease was truly horrific with the victims being struck first by boils, followed by prolonged bouts of vomiting blood and, mercifully, death, usually within three days. Highly contagious, it spread rapidly throughout Europe and hit northeastern Spain particularly hard. Although death statistics are not known, it decimated entire

The Iberian Peninsula during the 13th century.

The perfectly preserved medieval town of Besalú in Catalonia, which
remained an important settlement up until the 14th century.
The bridge dates from the 11th century.

populations, leaving farmland untended for want of laborers and villages emptied of their inhabitants.

No longer absorbed by military expansionism into Muslim territories, the attention of the kings now turned inwardly to the thorny issue of how to control an increasingly unruly nobility. As it attempted to keep its privileges, the intrigues and plots on the part of the nobility became so complex that it drew in members of the royal families themselves, leading to murderous rifts and disputes over succession.

This was exemplified by the notorious rule of Pedro I, the king of Castilla-León, whose ruthless and bloody reign from 1350 to 1369 earned him the nickname of the *El Cruel*. During his rule, rivalry between members of the Spanish royalty reached its murderous pinnacle as he fought his half-brother, Enrique de Trastámara, the bastard son of Alfonso XI and his lover Leonor de Guzmán. Like his predecessors, Pedro faced an unruly nobility that was determined to resist any attempts by the monarch to reduce its power. There was a great deal of discontent amongst the nobility at this time. Its members were experiencing serious economic losses owing to the shortage of farmhands to work their fields. Seeking to undermine Pedro's authority, a group of noblemen allied themselves with Enrique who managed to depose his half-brother. But Pedro was quick to regain his throne. The struggle reached its bitter conclusion as the two finally engaged in savage hand-to-hand combat— Pedro *El Cruel* was slain, stabbed in the chest by his half-brother.

Enrique II ascended to the throne, and so began the reign of the Trastámara dynasty. This was not the end of the troubles for Castilla, which descended into a long period of royal infighting and clashes with the nobility.

Enrique II was heavily indebted to his allies for his successful bid for the throne. He had called on France, which was ready to help on account of its displeasure over Pedro's desertion of his French wife, Princess Blanche; and also on Aragón, which was keen to exploit its neighbor's weakness. These allies, in addition to the nobility that supported him, needed to be rewarded generously.

The Alcázar of Segovia with a history dating back to
the 13th and 14th centuries.

All in all, it was a constant struggle for the royalty to keep the
nobility loyal. A content nobility, if indeed this was possible, was an
expensive business that could cost the monarchy well over half of its
income. It normally fell on the populace to shoulder the financial
burden through increased taxation.

## The Nobility, Townsfolk, and Peasants

For the peasants' life under the nobility was harsh. Noblemen and
ecclesiastical orders held vast areas of land, granted by the monarchs,
and were a law unto themselves. The civil and church lords took full
administrative control over their estates, which included collecting
taxes, appointing officials, and dispensing justice. Amongst
their privileges was the right to demand services and payment of dues
from their vassals. In Castilla, from the 13th century onwards, the
nobles adopted of the practice of passing property and land, called
*señoríos*, to the first-born son, which prevented the land being divided

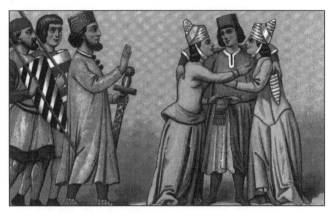

13th-century Christian soldiers and noblewomen wearing typical uniforms and costumes of the period.

amongst the different members of the family. Castilla now saw a considerable part of its territory concentrated in the hands of a few extremely powerful families who were not scared to challenge the authority of the king.

The relationship between the landed nobility and towns was similarly strained. A large number of towns were given special privileges and encouraged to develop a cooperative spirit. These towns formed the backbone of the reconquest and, for many years, remained like fortresses, braced for the likelihood of Muslim attacks. Merchants and artisans flourished, and craftsmen belonged to guilds that had a great degree of self-regulation. Around the towns were public lands, including woods, lakes, and rivers that the townsfolk had the right to use.

Predictably, given their strength, there was much abuse of power on the part of the nobility which attempted to exert its influence over the surrounding towns. Soon the the situation deteriorated. In response, towns began to organize themselves into *hermandades*, meaning "brotherhoods," to defend themselves against the nobles' excesses. Amongst other measures, the *hermandades* developed their own police force and, acquiring weapons, on occasion went so far as to engage in limited wars against the nobility. The *hermandades* were not unpopular with the monarchs, who were always happy to see overambitious aristocratic noses bloodied.

The 15th century brought with it a continuation of indiscipline on the part of the nobility, as well as bitter royal feuding over rights of succession to the throne. It was to take the efforts of two monarchs, Isabella I of Castilla and Fernando II of Aragón, to impose the absolute power of the monarchy over the nobility, and to unite the two kingdoms of Castilla and Aragón. Theirs was a rule of tremendous political change that heralded in a new age. It was from this point that the foundations of the modern Spanish nation state were laid.

# THE GOLDEN AGE OF SPAIN

## Isabella and Fernando—The Catholic Monarchs

In the 15th century, on October 19, 1469, the two young heirs to the
thrones of Castilla and Aragón were married in secret. Neither of the
two had met each other before that day. They were the 18-year-old
Isabella, half-sister of King Enrique IV of Castilla, and Fernando, still
only 17, the eldest son of King Juan of Aragón. Together they were to
be known as the Catholic Monarchs, and their reign is of immense
significance in the history of Spain.

As we have seen, Spain during the 15th century did not exist as a
single nation, nor was it a unified political unit. The Iberian Peninsula
was a patchwork collection of the kingdoms of Castilla, Aragón,
Catalonia, Navarra, Valencia, and the Muslim emirate of Granada—
each of which had its own identity. With the arrival of Isabella I and
Fernando V, the political make-up of the peninsula was to undergo
major changes. The political and legal foundations of the future Spanish
state were laid as the two monarchs began a process that united the
scattered kingdoms and opened the way for a period of history, between
1492 until the mid-17th century, known as the Golden Age of Spain.

From the beginning, Isabella and Fernando were to face many
difficulties. Their marriage had been conducted in secrecy owing to the
disapproval of King Enrique IV, who had been hopeful that she would
marry the king of Portugal, a man twice her age. Enrique IV's aim was
to stabilize and strengthen Castilla's unsteady relations with Portugal.
Yet, all along the young Isabella, admired at court for her beauty, had
had her sights set on marrying Fernando, an intelligent young man who
was heir to the second largest kingdom in Christian Spain—that of
Aragón, which had also acquired Italian possessions that included
Naples and Sicily. Her desire found a great deal of support among
influential nobles who stood to gain from closer ties between Castilla

Isabella and Fernando, the Catholic Monarchs who united Spain under the banner of Christianity.

and Aragón. Once married, the couple ran into further problems owing to the fact that they were second cousins. It was not until the pope ratified the marriage in December 1471, that the union became legitimate in the eyes of Christian world.

Although Isabella's right to the throne was, after some reluctance, finally acknowledged by King Enrique IV before his death, there were many who disagreed. Isabella faced strong opposition from those who held a girl called Juana to be the rightful heir to the throne. Juana, who was nine years younger than Isabella, was allegedly King Enrique IV's daughter; yet there was much debate over her true status—the king's opponents believed her to be the illegitimate child of his wife and a courtier.

Isabella was crowned Queen of Castilla on December 13, 1474, but it was to take another four years and the crowning of Fernando before her position was finally secured. A period of civil war followed her coronation,

Views of Segovia, where Isabella was crowned Queen of Castilla.

during which time she fought to bring the various factions and towns that opposed her under control. To do this, she counted on the vital support of her husband, who by now had shown himself to be highly adept in military matters.

Isabella also had to confront the serious risk posed by Portugal. In 1475, the Portuguese king, Alfonso V, had made clear his aim to invade Castilla, marry Juana, and place her on the Castilian throne. The following year, he sent his army over the border into Castilla; yet he was stopped by Isabella's troops, headed by Fernando, at the battle of Toro in 1476. A second attempt in 1478 was similarly unsuccessful. The following year, Castilla and Portugal called a truce and went to the negotiation table, and a lasting peace between the two kingdoms was established. Alfonso V renounced his claims to Castilla. As for Juana, she was sent to a monastery where she was to remain for the rest of her life, still convinced of her rightful claim to the throne.

## The Conquest of Granada

Fernando's accession to the throne of Aragón in 1479 finally put the two monarchs in a position to build upon the gains they had made and to strengthen the formidable partnership they had created as joint rulers of their kingdoms. Yet, it is important to emphasize that despite the union, the two kingdoms were still separate territories and the decision

The city of Granada, the last bastion of Islam in Spain. Nestling in the hills of the foreground is the Alhambra, a palace and fort complex built by the Muslims. In the background lie the snowcapped peaks of the Sierra Nevada, Spain's highest mountain range.

Sentry post looking out towards the Mediterranean Sea from the Muslim Gibralfaro Castle in Málaga. The city was conquered by the Catholic Monarchs in August 1487 as part of their campaign against the Kingdom of Granada.

to rule jointly was mutual. They were not contractually bound to give up any power of their kingdoms to the other.

Having successfully united their medieval kingdoms, the two monarchs were now free to unite forces and focus their attention on conquering the last stronghold of Islam on the peninsula. After a campaign that lasted ten years, Granada, described at the time by a contemporary Egyptian traveler as one of the "greatest and most beautiful cities," finally surrendered in 1492. The reconquest was thus accomplished, bringing an end to nearly eight centuries of Islamic civilization in Spain.

This event had far-reaching effects throughout Christian Europe, which now viewed the two monarchs with high regard. In recognition of their achievements, the pope gave them the title of the "Catholic Monarchs," or the *Reyes Católicos* as they are known in the Spanish language. Under the terms of the peace treaty, ratified by Isabella and Fernando, the Muslims were guaranteed, amongst many other things, full religious freedom and the right to continue to work and ply their trade. A period of relative calm followed in Granada, though within a few years the guarantees to leave the Muslims in peace were being deliberately ignored. After initial unsuccessful attempts by the Catholic Church to peacefully convert Muslims, it began to bring pressure on Isabella and Fernando to allow heavy-handed tactics to bring new souls into the Church. By the end of the century, most of the Muslim leaders had left for North Africa and abandoned the rest of the Islamic population to the mercy of their new Christian overlords. Those who who stayed were faced with the choice of converting to Christianity or expulsion; and the monarchy had at its disposal a highly effective means of helping them them decide—the Spanish Inquisition.

## The Spanish Inquisition and the Expulsion of the Jews

The Spanish Inquisition has passed into history as one of the most notorious and ruthless institutions, responsible for countless atrocities carried out in the name of Christianity. Introduced into Spain with the blessing of Isabella in 1481, its first unfortunate victims were Jewish converts to Christianity. It became a weapon of the state, which was used to stamp out dissent and impose religious uniformity across the country.

Under Muslim rule in Al-Andalus, the Jews had been allowed to live in peace for centuries; and it was only with the invasion of the fundamentalist Almohad Berbers in 1146 that many were forced to flee to the northern Christian-held territories. Here they found safety amongst their Jewish brethren, who had enjoyed relative peace and prosperity. In fact, many had risen to prominent positions in the Christian royal courts and other institutions. Yet, their fortunes

14th-century Hebrew tablet in the Jewish Quarter of Barcelona which reads: "Holy Foundation of Rabbi Samuel Hassardi for whom life never ends."

began to change as anti-Semitism reared its ugly head in the mid-14th century. Caught up in the complex politics of the feuding royalty and nobility, they were the focus of anti-Jewish pogroms on several occasions. In 1391, a wave of brutal attacks against Jews began in Sevilla and soon spread around Castilla. Thousands of Jews were killed in its wake. The climate of fear led to the mass conversion of Jews, known as *conversos*, to Christianity.

Initially spared from the prejudices aimed at Jews, a number of *converso* families became highly influential and went on to play key roles in the governing of the state, as well as the running of the Church. Furthermore, the recent converts had begun intermarrying old

For some unfortunate victims of the Spanish Inquisition, torture was followed by burning at the stake.

*Below*: Scenes of torture during the Spanish Inquisition.

Christian families, with the result that even the royal Trastámara family had Jewish blood in its veins.

Yet it was not too long before the *conversos* fell foul of the politics of the time. The situation became more serious as various anti-Jewish groups began to question the sincerity of the *conversos*, and linked Jewish ancestry with the idea of racial impurity. This "taint," they argued, disqualified the new Christians from certain posts. Things began to look rather precarious for the Jews and *conversos*. With the ascendency of Isabella to the throne, their fortunes were to change very much for the worse.

Isabella, whose religious piety bordered on fanaticism, initially introduced the Inquisition into Castilla in order to investigate the "suspect" converts. The Catholic Inquisition was not new to Europe. It had been established by Pope Gregory IX in 1231 to combat heretics. The purpose was to "inquire" into the beliefs of those who did not conform to the Catholic Church, and to try show them their "error" of their ways. Whereas the Inquisition was in theory carried out under the watchful eye of the Vatican, the Spanish version, although given the

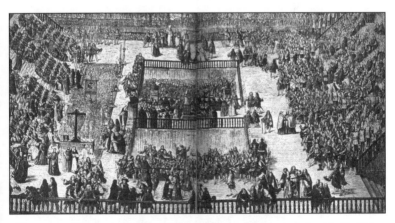

The mass punishment of victims of the Inquisition publicly carried out in Madrid's Plaza Mayor during the 17th century.

One of the narrow alleyways in the heart of the well-preserved Medieval Jewish Quarter of Girona, Catalonia.

blessing of the pope, was directly controlled by the Spanish Monarchy. Free to choose who they wanted to implement the Inquisition, it swiftly became an effective weapon for Isabella and Fernando to fight all those who might challenge their authority. Soon the desires of Catholic Monarchs for a unified country meant that all subjects had to accept one religion—the religion of the State.

The man who organized and headed the Spanish Inquisition was a Spanish Dominican monk by the name of Tomás de Torquemada, confessor to Isabella and Fernando. A fanatic by all accounts, Grand Inquisitor Torquemada set about investigating both Jewish and Muslim converts, as well as those suspected of heresy. Those who were accused (exactly by whom they were not told) faced the prospect of tortures that were so horrific that they have since become legendary. Amongst the many terrifying instruments employed to extract confessions were the rack, thumbscrews, and knee-splitters. Unfortunate victims might find themselves winched to the ceiling by ropes attached to the wrist and with heavy weights secured to their feet. From there they would be dropped to within a few feet of the floor resulting in dislocation of the limbs. Once found guilty, the Church washed its hands of the affair, and handed the victims to the civil authorities for punishment. For some, the whole ordeal ended in death, by burning at the stake. The Spanish state, in an extreme display of its absolute authority, benefitted twice over. Not only did it demonstrate its power over dissenters, it also amassed a fortune in confiscated property.

In 1492—the same year as the surrender of Granada that brought the whole of the Iberian Peninsula under Christian rule—the Catholic Monarchs decided to rid themselves of Jews altogether. All Jews were ordered to leave Castilla and Aragón within four months, or suffer the penalty of death. Although many chose conversion, only to face the onslaught of the Inquisition, there was a huge exodus. Exactly how many left the country is not known, but estimates range from 60,000 to more than 150,000.

The Muslims of Granada fared little better. Those who chose to convert to Christianity, or *moriscos* as they were they were now called, also became targets of the Inquisition. Under their new overlords, the Muslims had to take great care not to arouse suspicions that they were secretly practising their old religion—even taking a bath could be considered cause enough to bring in the dreaded Inquisitor.

It was a far cry from the days when Spain, under the rule of the Muslim caliphs, had been famous for its tolerance and learning. Where books were once collected and valued, they were now heaped into piles on the streets and burned in the name of Christianity. The Inquisition proved to be a durable institution, and it was only officially terminated in 1834.

## The Colonization of the New World

The year 1492 also marked one of the most significant events in history, the voyage of Christopher Columbus to the New World. Columbus, known to the Spanish speaking world as Cristóbal Colón, was of Italian (Geonoese) origin and had for years dreamed of finding a westward spice-route to Asia by sailing across the Atlantic Ocean. It was Isabella and Fernando who listened to his wild plans and sponsored his expedition. On August 3, Columbus set out from the Andalusian port of Palos with his three ships and headed west. In the early hours of the morning on October 12, 1492, they sighted land. It turned out not to be Asia, but one of the islands in the Bahamas, which Columbus named San Salvador. He had inadvertantly stumbled on lands previous unknown to Europeans—which of course came to be known as the Americas. The European discovery was to fundamentally change the course of Spanish and world history, and lead to devastating results for the civilizations and cultures of the New World.

Christopher Columbus's sighting of the Americas led the way to wholesale colonization of the Americas by the Spanish. Christian Spain had been built on the conquest and colonization of Muslim territories, a fact that had shaped the politics and culture of its people. It is no surprise, therefore, that this profoundly influenced the subsequent conquest and colonization of the New World, which was carried out through the persuasive marriage of the sword and the cross.

The tomb of Christopher Columbus in Sevilla.

The early stages of colonization took place in a haphazard manner. The first to arrive were the Conquistadors, willing to risk their lives for gold and other riches that might be found in the New World. Their ultimate aim was to secure for themselves the life of a nobleman. As they began to explore the mainland of the New World, they found not only the small huntergatherer tribes but also highly sophisticated

Maya, Inca, and Aztec civilizations. Accompanied by only a very few men, and in the face of severe hardship and privation, the Conquistadors gained a foothold in the new land. The most ambitious of them—men such as Hernán Cortés and Francisco Pizarro, who brought down the Aztec and Inca Empires respectively—used guile and deceit to make up for their lack of military power, exploiting divisions within indigenous societies to turn one political faction against another with devasting effect. This was amply demonstrated by Pizarro, who conquered the Inca empire in Peru with just 180 men and 27 horses.

Soon the Spanish Crown began to assert its authority over its new overseas territories. The Spanish Indies were divided into two viceroyalties (and later into four), each with its own viceroy. The viceroyalty of New Spain covered the territory north of the Panamanian Isthmus and was governed from Mexico City. To the south, the Spanish territories in South America were governed from Lima, the capital of the viceroyalty of Peru. All government appointments in the Americas from the viceroys down were appointed by the Crown. In order to keep a tight rein over the region, the most important posts were usually reserved for those born in Spain.

The Indies became a huge source of wealth for Spain, as vast quantities of gold and silver were shipped across the Atlantic. It was this wealth that was to enable Spain to fund its costly wars in Europe, which were waged in an attempt to maintain its role as the dominant European power. Even when the Crown coffers were empty, it was able to use the promise of silver from its colonies to secure bank loans. For three centuries, the Spanish state imposed a strict trade monopoly over commerce in the Indies. The colonies were prevented from trading with foreigners, and the flow of imports and exports were channelled through a handful of official ports in Spain and the New World. This took place under the watchful eye of the state regulatory body in Seville, the *Casa de Contratación*, which controlled every aspect of transatlantic trade from inspecting ships to collecting taxes and duties.

# Carlos I of Spain and the Hapsburgs

Despite the successes of Isabella and Fernando, they were no more able control the hand of fate when it came to succession than their predecessors. Their only son died before them at the early age of 21. Their daughter Juana, who subsequently became queen after Isabella's death in 1504, became mentally unstable. She was married to Felipe of Austria, a member of the Austrian royal Hapsburg family and son of Maximilian I, the Holy Roman Emperor. For two years they ruled Castilla, but then tragedy struck. Felipe died unexpectedly; and Juana, who was already known to be emotionally vulnerable, went into shock and even refused to let her husband's coffin be taken from her. She became too mentally unstable to rule and had to be restricted to the confines of a castle.

The next in line to the throne was Carlos, Juana and Felipe's six-year-old son. Until he was old enough to ascend the throne, Fernando, who still remained king of Aragón, governed as regent of Castilla. There were many who opposed him and Fernando had to use of all his skills to keep the situation under control.

Upon Fernando's death in 1516, Carlos I inherited the thrones of Castilla and Aragón, the latter of which included territories in Italy as well as the Mediterranean islands of Sardinia and Sicily. Added to this were possessions that his mother had acquired in the Netherlands. The young 17-year-old king had never set foot in Spain before, and could not speak a word of Spanish. He immediately ran into problems with his new subjects. Every inch a foreigner in Spain, Carlos I surrounded himself with Flemish advisers who set about the task of administering Spain, handing over key posts to non-Spaniards in the process. The Spanish were mortified.

The new king then ran into trouble with his subjects over his bid to succeed his grandfather Maximilian as Holy Roman Emperor. His grandfather's death in 1519 had given him the Austrian throne, but he would have to compete against Henry VIII of England and Francis I of France for the title of Emperor. It was a prestigious position to hold and one that would make him ruler of a complex network of European territories that had been under the rule of Frankish and German kings since the crowning of the the first emperor, Charlemagne, in 800AD. Carlos I needed huge sums of money, which he borrowed from a major European bank, to pay off those whose influence would secure him his election.

His bid was successful, yet he was now in need of further funds to cover a trip to Central Europe in order to attend his coronation, which he intended to secure from the the state coffers of Castilla. He put his plan before a parliament convened in Santiago de Compostela, but at first his subjects refused. It was only finally granted, amidst much haggling and bitterness, after Carlos I pulled out all the stops to use his influence to secure the sum he needed.

Carlos I duly set off and in his absence left the affairs of governing the country in the hands of a foreigner, Adrian of Utrecht. This act was the last straw. Adrian was left to face the anger of the population and, before long, had a full-scale rebellion on his hands. Key cities in Castilla rose up against what they saw as their king's willingness to put the interests of the empire before those of Spain. And what really riled the rebels was the fact that they were expected to foot the bill. Joining forces, the *comuneros*, as they became known, signed a pact called the Holy Junta, proclaiming Queen Juana as the only authority in Spain. It was an honor that the mentally disturbed queen declined. The *comuneros*, as they became known, soon fell into disunity. The nobility, alarmed at the spread of movements opposed to "seigneurialism"—the feudal-like system that was the basis of their power—played it safe and joined forces with the monarchy. In 1521, after soundly defeating the *comuneros* at the Battle of Villalar and executing 23 of their leaders, Carlos I managed to reassert the authority of the Crown.

The uprising in Castilla coincided with a full-blown social rebellion in Valencia and Mallorca in the kingdom of Aragón. Amidst worsening social and economic conditions brought about by rising taxes and rents, grain shortages and attacks by pirates, various sectors of the population, including the middle classes and guilds, rose up in arms against the abuses of the nobility. The protest spread to other parts of the kingdom, and threatened to turn into a wholesale popular uprising. The Royal Army came down firmly on the side of the nobility and peace was finally restored.

Carlos I had now become Carlos V, Holy Roman Emperor and head of one of the largest empires the world had ever seen. Spain was launched into the international arena, and much of the responsibility of maintaining the imperial order in Europe now fell on the Spanish kingdoms, especially Castilla—and it was to be a costly business.

Spain's main enemy was France. Its king, Francis I, still smarting at his failure to secure the Imperial Crown, was not content to play second fiddle to Spain. His designs to increase his country's power in Europe by controlling the Italian peninsula exploded into conflict between France and Spain. In 1525, Carlos V's forces defeated the French at the Battle of Pavia in northern Italy. Francis I was taken prisoner and whisked away to Madrid, where he was forced to agree to renounce all claims to Italy. Once free, however, it was not long before he was again seeking to further France's ambitions in Europe and keeping Carlos V and Spain involved in further costly wars.

Under Carlos V, Spain was drawn into other major foreign disputes and conflicts, which put ever more strain on the country's limited resources. Tensions between Catholics and Protestants, especially in Germany, were a continuous source of trouble that thwarted attempts to impose Christian unity in Europe and undermined the security of Carlos V's Empire. Another threat came from the east, as the Muslim Ottoman Empire carried out a campaign of expansion. In a disturbing development Ottoman troops marched all the way to Vienna, the center of the Hapsburg's power. For a moment they had seemed poised to march into the European heartland, but they were soon driven back. Despite this failure, however, they continued to remain a threat to the security to the Imperial Crown.

Carlos V's rule represented a pinnacle in Spanish history. Spain had become the unquestionable dominant power in Europe—a situation that the king had actively and tirelessly fought to bring about.

Yet towards the end of the turbulent years of his reign, his energies began to wane. Carlos V thus abdicated as Holy Roman Emperor and then king of Spain. He finally retired to a monastery where he died in 1558. Prior to Carlos V's death, the throne of Spain had gone to his son Felipe; while his Imperial Crown had been bequeathed to his brother, Fernando. Thus the Hapsburgs were split into two branches.

## St. Teresa of Ávila and St. John of the Cross—
## Two Leading Lights in the World of Catholic Mysticism

In a land where the new ruling classes based their legitimacy on their championing of the Christian faith, 16th-century Spain held no room for religious deviation. This was not to say that there were no tensions within the Church. Indeed, two of the most influential figures in Christian mystical literature found themselves at odds with the religious establishment. These were Santa Teresa de Jesús (St. Teresa of Ávila) and San Juan de la Cruz (St. John of the Cross), who together dedicated their lives to reforming the religious order to which they belonged—the Carmelites.

Teresa Sánchez de Cepeda y Ahumada was born into a well-to-do *converso* family on March 28, 1515, in Ávila. From an early age Teresa was drawn to religion and began to showed an unusual pious streak. At the age of seven, she was so impressed by reading about the lives of the saints that she felt compelled to run away from home, accompanied by her brother Rodrigo, in search of Muslims to convert and ultimate martyrdom in service of God. Fortunately, her plans were thwarted by her uncle, who stopped them at the city gate.

Teresa was 20 when she first entered a monastery in Ávila belonging to the Carmelites—a religious order founded in Palestine in the 12th century and which, by the 16th century, had spread throughout Europe. Bad health, which blighted her throughout her life, forced her back to her family for a while, but she later returned. As the years went by Teresa began feel dissatisfied with the order which, with its lax rules, was not conducive towards the intensely spiritual life she was beginning to lead. Teresa wanted to see a return to the 'primitive rule', which prescribed a life of extreme ascetisism, poverty, and solitude. She soon embarked on a mission to reform the order and founded the Discalced (Barefoot) Carmelites. Together with Juan de la Cruz, she was responsible for the opening numerous houses around the country for nuns and friars in which the "primitive rule" was strictly enforced.

Her efforts brought her into direct confrontation with her superiors. who feared the power of the formidable "roving nun," as they called her, to upset the established order. There were attempts to

St. Teresa of Ávila.

put an end to her ambitions by deporting her to the Americas, but with the help of powerful friends in the Church, including the support of the Jesuits, she was able to continue her work traveling across the country and spreading her message.

It was Teresa's gift as a spiritual writer, however, that has earned her a special place in Western European history. Her works have become recognized as masterpieces of Spanish prose. Amongst them is the book entitled *The Interior Castle*, written while she was confined to Toledo by the Carmelite authorities. Inspired by her visions, Teresa describes a life of contemplation and the path towards mystical union with God.

Teresa's contempory and fellow mystic San Juan de la Cruz was born Juan de Yepes y Álvarez, in Fontiveros, Ávila, in 1542. Juan's father came from a wealthy family, but his decision to marry a poor weaver girl led to his being disinherited from the family fortune. Falling on hard times, the married couple struggled hard to bring up their three sons, of whom Juan was the youngest. Shortly after his birth, Juan's father died, leaving his mother fending desperately for the family. Yet Juan managed to receive a basic education at a school for the poor. At the age of 17, whilst working in a plague hospital, he was permitted to study under the Jesuits. Convinced of his calling he joined the Carmelites at the age of 20 and continued his studies at the University of Salamanca. He earned himself a reputation as an outstanding scholar and was soon ordained. It was around this time that he met Teresa. Like Teresa, Juan was dissatisfied with the laxity of the Carmelites and wanted to leave, but she persuaded him to stay and devote his energies to reforming the order—it was the start of a formidable partnership.

Juan was made spiritual director of Teresa's convent in Ávila and went on to play a key role in the movement to reform the order. The Carmelite authorities did not take too kindly to his activities and imprisoned him in Toledo in 1577. It was here, in solitary confinement that he wrote the first of three poems, "The Spiritual Canticle," which along with "Ascent of Mount Carmel," and "The Living Flame of Love", is considered a masterpiece of Western religious mystical literature. Up until his death in 1591, Juan continued to be persecuted by the religious authorities. Yet, both he and Teresa have since become highly revered saints in the Catholic world.

# Felipe II

With Felipe II's reign came a change to the style of royal government in Spain. Although he kept close ties with the German line of the Hapsburgs, he was very much a Spanish king. Unlike his cosmopolitan father who had spent much of his time traveling and actively participating in wars, Felipe II prefered to stay at home. He chose Madrid as his new capital because of its central location. It became the base from which, surrounded by a cadre of bureaucrats, he controlled his kingdom.

To his supporters, Felipe II was man of integrity with deeply-held religious convictions who took his role as a Catholic Monarch earnestly. To his Prostestant enemies, he was a ruthless, vengeful fanatic who would stop at nothing to further his own ends.

The Prostestant problem, which Felipe II inherited from his father, was to be a continuous thorn in the Crown's side. It was the source of great conflict that created a continuous drain on royal finances and military power. After his father's abdication, part of Felipe II's inheritance had been territories in the Netherlands, which formed a loose collection of Catholic and Protestant provinces. Whereas Carlos V had dealt with these possessions and the Protestants with great care to avoid upsetting the order in Europe, his son approached the matter differently. Felipe II treated the Netherlands as an extension of Spain, and acted accordingly. After a period of highly unpopular policies in the region, which resulted in economic crisis that was exacerbated by high taxes levied by the Crown, the king rapidly found himself highly unpopular.

Matters soon got seriously out of hand when, in 1566, Felipe II decided to halt the progress of the Protestant Reformation. Protests, initially centered on concerns over religious freedom, gave way to violent uprisings sparked by economic and social conditions. The king responded by appointing a fanatical general, the Duke of Alba, who set about crushing any signs of rebellion and established a reign of terror known as the Council of Blood. Under the new tyrannical regime, more than a thousand people were sentenced to death. In addition to the creation of punitive taxes to pay for the cost of the conflict, anti-Protestant laws were enforced and heavy fines imposed. It was a recipe for disaster. After two much respected counts, Egmont and Hornes, were publicly beheaded for treason, dissatisfaction and rebellion against the Spanish crown became uncontainable. By 1568, it had spread to other parts of the Netherlands.

This marked the beginning of conflict in the area that would last another 80 years and incur expenses that would, time and again, bleed the debt-ridden Spanish Crown dry. That it managed to survive was thanks to the constant supply of gold and silver from its mines in the Americas, which it used as collateral to cover the huge amounts it borrowed.

It was under Felipe II that the episode of the famous Spanish "Invincible" Armada took place—an almost legendary event in the

The public executions of Egmont and Hornes in Brussels, 1568.
Their deaths caused outrage in the Netherlands and added
greatly to Felipe II's unpopularity in the region.

histories of Spain and England. It happened after Felipe II declared war on Queen Elizabeth I of England. This declaration was partly a response to the continuous attacks on ships bringing Spanish gold from the Americas by English buccaneers such as Francis Drake and John Hawkins, as well as to the English support for the Protestant rebels in the Netherlands. Felipe II spent a fortune putting together the huge Spanish Armada (*armada* is Spanish for "navy") with the aim of invading England. It was a spectacular disaster. In August 1588, the Armada was intercepted by English ships and in its retreat around the British Isles, it ran into fearsome storms resulting in utter devastation—few ships returned home. It was a tremendous loss of face for the Spanish that put an end to its hopes of naval superiority, a reputation subsequently enjoyed by the English.

The beautiful city of Lisbon, Portugal, seen from the River Tejo (Tagus)—once part of Spain and where Felipe II constructed a royal palace.

The monastery of San Lorenzo del Escorial, near Madrid, built on the orders of Felipe II as a final resting place the Spanish monarchs, and where he himself was buried.

If there was little to rejoice about when it came to the rest of Europe, the addition of Portugal to the Spanish Crown in 1580 was a dream come true for Spain. For the Spanish this was the unity that mattered—the whole of the Iberian Peninsula under the rule of one Catholic Monarch. Felipe II, whose mother was Princess Isabel of Portugal, had gained the throne by chance of his lineage: after the death of the young Portuguese king, Sebastian, Felipe was a legitimate contender for the disputed succession. In order to prevent rival claims, Felipe, certainly not the first choice of the Portuguese, left nothing to chance and marched an army into Portugal proclaiming himself king. To this day the Portuguese look back on their days as part of Spain with a hint of good-natured rivalry—best summed up by the saying: *"Nem bom vento, nem bom casamento,"* roughly translated as "neither a good wind nor a good marriage ever came from Spain."

As Felipe II grew older, he was dogged by ill health. Plagued by gout the king was often confined to his bed. The last year of his life was spent in agony as sores and abcesses broke out all over his body. So that he could spend the last days of his life in the monastery of El Escorial, some 32 miles from Madrid, the king was carried in a specially designed chair by his attendants. The arduous uphill journey took four days in the blazing summer heat of June 1598. Felipe II died in El Escorial, after nearly two months on his back, and in such agony from his open sores that his attendants could not move him even to change his clothes or bed linen.

Felipe II's basilica, El Escorial.

## El Greco—Master Painter of Toledo

One of the greatest artists of the Spanish Golden Age, El Greco, was not in fact from Spain, but was lured to Spanish shores in the hope of receiving a commission from Felipe II to work at El Escorial. El Greco, whose name means "The Greek," was born Domenikos Theotokopoulos, in 1541, on the island of Crete. A well-educated man, he went to Venice in the mid-1560s and studied in the workshops of his teacher Titian

Titian was an an enormously influential Italian painter, famous for his religious and mythological works, and also an important figure in Spanish history on account of his work commissioned by Carlos V. Amongst his masterpieces is a majestic portrait of the king on horseback wearing a suit of armor, intended to commemorate his victory over the Protestants at the Battle of Mühlberg. Another of his greatest works is a portrait of Felipe II, painted while he was still a prince at the age of 23.

After spending several years with Titian, El Greco moved to Rome, where he continued to absorb Italian influences and was greatly inspired by another Italian master, Michelangelo. Only when he was in his mid-thirties did he finally settle in Spain. Yet El Greco failed to impress the king, who had been employing Italian artists to embellish El Escorial and had expected a quite different style from a student of Titian.

Although snubbed by the Spanish monarchy, El Greco was nevertheless able to build himself a reputation that enabled him to remain in Spain. Establishing himself in Toledo, where he lived and worked until his death in 1614, he produced an extraordinarily powerful body of work employing his own unique style—filling his canvases with elongated human forms and using color to dramatic effect. Much of his work was commissioned for churches in the region, and, to this day, Toledo has become synonymous with the great artist, whose paintings are spread throughout the city.

El Greco's signature. Despite living in Spain he continued to sign his name in Greek.

## Felipe III

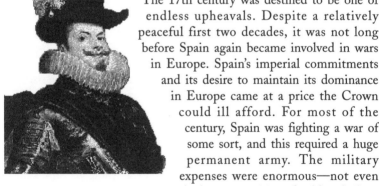

Felipe III.

With Felipe II's death came the end of the century and a new king, in the shape of his son Felipe III. The 17th century was destined to be one of endless upheavals. Despite a relatively peaceful first two decades, it was not long before Spain again became involved in wars in Europe. Spain's imperial commitments and its desire to maintain its dominance in Europe came at a price the Crown could ill afford. For most of the century, Spain was fighting a war of some sort, and this required a huge permanent army. The military expenses were enormous—not even the huge quantities of gold and silver

Monument to Felipe III in the Plaza Mayor of Madrid.

from the Americas, which now went straight to the bankers to pay off debts, were enough to meet the astronomical cost. To tackle the problem, the monarchy created new taxes—never a popular measure—and raised money by selling noble titles, knighthoods, ecclesiastical posts, and even towns, which had the adverse effect of transferring power away from the monarchy to the ever powerful nobility and Church.

The economy in 17th-century Spain was in a dreadful state. Agriculture was hit by a succession of bad harvests. What little industry existed in Spain was in a similarly desperate predicament. The textile industry, which was based on wool, suffered heavily on account of rampant inflation in the country. Foreign manufacturers were buying raw material from Spain and selling the finished products back to the Spanish at prices cheaper than their own products.

To add to the country's difficulties, its population was severely reduced by famine and epidemics of bubonic plague. During one epidemic, Sevilla lost almost half of its inhabitants. The population drain was exacerbated by the number of men who left the country to fight in wars, while others sought their fortune in the Americas. Added to this was Felipe III's decision to expel the population of *moriscos* from Valencia in 1609. These unfortunate people, who had been forced to convert to Christianity, had long been accused of continuing to practice Islam in secret. Most were were skilled farmers, and their loss was devasting to the region's economy. The following year, the rest of *moriscos* inhabiting other parts of the country were also ordered to leave—in all, as many as 300,000 were thrown out of Spain.

The Andalusian-style town of Chechauoen, in the Rif Mountains of Morocco—founded by some of the earlier Spanish Muslims to flee Spain in the 15th century.

In the face of the onset of social and economic hardship, the Royal Court embarked on a period of fanciful wrecklessness. Little relishing the prospects of getting to grips with the complexities of government, Felipe III from the beginning handed over the governing of the country to a chief minister, the Duke of Lerma. The Duke promptly set about squandering the Crown's money and oversaw a period of financial ruin, decadence, and corruption. In a massive display of pomp, the court embarked on a series of extravagent banquets and receptions the likes of which had never been seen before.

## Cervantes and *Don Quixote*

Despite the upheavals of Felipe III's reign, it also saw coincided with the life of one of Spain's greatest writers, Miguel de Cervantes Saavedra. Cervantes was born in Alcalá de Henares, near Madrid, in 1547 (probably on September 29). His novel, *Don Quixote*, published in 1605, is considered throughout the world to be a masterpiece and has been translated into more than sixty languages. The novel, which is a parody of the tales of chivalry that abounded at the time, recounts the adventures that befall an elderly man who sets out to live the romantic life of a knight-errant in the company of his squire Sancho Panza.

Cervantes own life was full of adventure. He fought in the war against the Turks in the Battle of Lepanto in 1571, during which Christian forces put an end to the threat of Ottoman naval supremacy in the Mediterranean. Cervantes was wounded and left with permanent injuries to his left hand, and on his return he was taken prisoner by the Turks. Five years

Miguel de Cervantes, author of *Don Quixote*—regarded as a masterpiece throughout the world.

later and after four attempted escapes, he was finally released and returned to Madrid. During the course of his life, Cervantes wrote many works including novels, plays, and poems. He died in Madrid on April 23, 1616.

## Felipe IV

Upon his death in 1621, Felipe III was succeeded by his son, Felipe IV. Like his father, Felipe IV entrusted the governing of Spain to another man. His first minister was the Count Duke of Olivares, an ambitious politician who set himself the task of putting Spain back on track as the undisputed dominant power in Europe. With Olivares at the helm, Spain launched energetically into the series of conflicts in Europe that lasted between 1618 and 1648 and became known as the Thirty Years War, whose aim was to consolidate the power of the Hapsburgs.

As for the governing of Spain itself, Olivares proposed no less than that the whole country be governed by one law and adopt the institutions of Castilla—thus doing away with the differences caused by the various privileges enjoyed by the regions. One of Olivares's major projects was the ill-fated *Unión de Armas* (Union of Arms). Up until now, Castilla had borne the brunt of Spain's military obligations. Olivares therefore proposed that all the kingdoms and provinces of the Spanish Crown should contribute to a huge collective army that would number some 140,000. It was by no means a dream shared by all. Few were prepared to give up their jealously-guarded freedoms and fiscal autonomy. In Aragón, for example, there were laws that prevented the recruitment of troops for conflicts outside the kindom. Quite apart from the unpopular prospect of fighting in overseas wars, the increase in taxes to pay for such an army was enough to cause widespread hostility towards the meddling Olivares.

In Catalonia, anti-Castilian feeling was rife and tensions mounted over the presence of Castilian troops deployed in the Catalonian region of the Pyrenees. These had been stationed there to secure the region from the clutches of France, which had recently declared war on Spain. But the Catalans were keen to see the back of them. Soon the Crown had a full-scale rebellion on its hands. On June 12, 1640, there was a popular uprising in Barcelona, in which crowds attacked and killed Castilian government officials and assassinated the governor. Before long the drama had escalated into a civil war, in the course of which the French intervened and placed the region under its protection. It was to be several years before the Spanish Crown was once again able to regain the territory and impose its authority over the land. Felipe IV, keen to avoid a repeat performance, found it necessary to placate the Catalans by swearing to uphold and respect the privileges that they had traditionally enjoyed.

Revolt was not limited to Catalonia. In Andalucía, in 1641, the Marquis of Ayamonte and the Duke of Medina-Sidonia attempted to establish an independent state with Sevilla as its capital. In Aragón, in 1648, the Duke of Híjar similarly and vainly hoped to carve out an independent kingdom with himself as king.

Portugal, on the other hand, was more successful. A secessionist movement had led to open revolt against the unpopular Spanish monarchy; and in 1640, the Portuguese successfully won their independence and proclaimed Juan IV as their new king.

Meanwhile, in Spain popular urban discontent was becoming increasingly unmanageable as a result of heavy taxes and the high cost of food. Olivares's situation was no longer tenable. His unpopular policies aimed at imposing the cast-iron rule of the monarchy over the country had stirred the cauldron of discontent and resulted in little more than one crisis after another, both at home and abroad. In 1643, his career in ruins, he was forced to stand down as the king's minister.

Yet the disasters continued. In 1648, after a series of military defeats, Spain was forced to recognize the independence of Holland and accept the fact that France was now the new dominant power in Europe. Further battles against France, now joined by the English, ended in defeat. Over the next sixty years, Spain's remaining possessions in Europe were lost one by one. The final blow came in 1713, when it surrendered control over its Italian territories—including Milan, Naples, Sardinia, and Sicily.

When Felipe IV died in 1665, he left his foundering and bankrupt kingdom to his sickly four-year-old son, Carlos II. A regency followed, until, at the age of fourteen, Carlos II was declared old enough to assume his role as king. Yet the enfeebled king, known as *El Hechizado* (The Bewitched), was given little to do as various ministers took over the governing of Spain. There followed a period of uncertainty and further wars, made all the more worse by the fact that the king's ill health prevented him from producing an heir to throne. He died childless at the age of forty in November 1700.

## Velázquez

While El Greco was unsuccessful in his attempt to gain the patronage of the monarchy, Diego Velázquez, another outstanding painter of the Golden Age, had the good fortune to find a sympathetic champion in his king, Felipe IV.

Velázquez was born in Seville in 1599. He was well-educated and developed a passion for painting at a young age. His early career was spent creating still-life paintings of objects—such as kitchen utensils, fruit, birds, fish, and human heads—in darkened studios, known as *bodegones*. In his early twenties, Veláquez arrived in Madrid, hoping to gain the patronage of the king. Although not successful the first time, he soon got his opportunity after painting the monarch's portrait. Felipe IV was so impressed by Velázquez that he appointed him a court painter, and would remain his patron for life. The two became friends and Felipe IV even had a key to Velázquez's workshop, where he would often enjoy sitting and watching him paint.

Veláquez went on to become one of the greatest painters of the 17th century, and his paintings of the king, royal family, and courtiers offer a wonderful and valuable glimpse into the royal household at the time. One of his masterpieces, entitled *Las Meninas* (*Maids of Honor*), showing the little princess Margarita with her attendants, a dwarf, and a dog, has often been described as the greatest painting in the world. As an artist, his technique was second to none, and his ability to capture the likeness of his sitters led Pope Innocent X, after seeing his image captured by the masterful Velázquez, to remark that the portrait was "too truthful."

Always on friendly terms with the king, Velázquez was given a number of responsibilities in addition to his role as court painter. Later in life he became chamberlain of the palace, which involved arranging the royal apartments and organizing journeys made by the king. Yet, Velázquez spent his life attempting to gain the same status of other courtiers. Being an artist, he worked with his hands, and, therefore, was expected to sit in the lower ranks with the likes of servants of the nobility at public events. However, towards the end of his life, he succeeded in achieving the ultimate honor. In 1659, despite opposition from the nobility, the king knighted him. The following year, Velázquez died, leaving behind a body of work that has withstood the passage of time and includes some of the finest paintings to be found in the world. Today the largest collection of his works is housed at the Prado Museum, in Madrid—including *Las Meninas*.

# SPAIN UNDER THE BOURBONS

## The War of the Spanish Succession

The death of Carlos II saw the end of the rule of the Hapsburgs in Spain and heralded in a new dynasty—the royal house of the French Bourbons. Before he died, the childless and brotherless king had taken the advice of his Council of State and named the Duke of Anjou as his heir. Philip of Anjou was a member of the House of Bourbon, the ruling French dynasty and the grandson of Louis XIV of France. The decision was the result of much negotiating between the Spanish and the French, who potentially stood to gain much. Philip of Anjou made his entry into Madrid in 1701 to be crowned Felipe V, King of Spain.

The installation of the Bourbons was seen by some countries as a major threat to the balance of power in Europe. Neither the Austrians, English, or Dutch were keen to see the creation of a new French super-state—which would happen if Felipe also took over the French throne after his grandfather's death. Instead, they favored a continuation of the Hapsburg dynasty in Spain. Accordingly, their choice for the Spanish throne was a Hapsburg, Charles, the Archduke of Austria and son of the Austrian Emperor Leopold I. War immediately broke out in various parts of Europe between the two opposing factions—those who supported Felipe V, and those who backed Charles.

Within a short time, the fighting had spread to the Iberian Peninsula and Spain descended into civil war. Castilla largely came out in support of Felipe V, while Aragón leaned towards Charles. Known as the War of the Spanish Succession, the conflict raged on from 1702 to 1714. Spain was reduced to little more than a battlefield in which the various powers of Europe bloodily pursued their own interests.

The war came to an end in 1713 with the signing of the Treaty of Utrecht, the terms of which the Spanish only little influenced. The supporters of Archduke Charles, now somewhat wary after he had succeeded to the Imperial Crown (which together with the Spanish Crown would have given him a great deal of power in Europe) agreed to recognize Felipe V as king of Spain. Yet to prevent the possibility of a union between Spain and France, Felipe V was forced to renounce any claims to the French throne, a prohibition that also extended to his heirs.

Furthermore, Spain lost the territories of Gibraltar and the Balearic island of Menorca to the British, the Netherlands to Holland, and Sicily to Savoy. The following year in the Treaty of Rastatt, Spain was stripped of its Italian possessions of Naples, Sardinia, and Milan. The days when Spain was a major power in Europe were over—Spain had truly become a mere shadow of its former glorious self.

## Felipe V—The Reluctant King

Like Carlos I almost two centuries before him, the new Bourbon king first set foot in Spain at the age of seventeen and could not speak a word of Spanish. He too brought with him an entourage of advisers, in this case from France, who were responsible for importing many French customs to the Royal Court.

Felipe V's reign ushered in a process of centralization on a scale never before seen. At this time, the various regions of Spain continued to enjoy various privileges that allowed them a great degree of politcal and fiscal autonomy. Known as *fueros*, these became the target of his government, which set about imposing a unified political, legal, and fiscal system modelled on that of Castilla. Only Navarra and the Basque country were able to maintain their *fueros*, a reward for their loyalty to the Bourbon Crown during the War of Succession. From now on, Castilla would no longer bear the brunt of the costs of running the state. This burden would be shared with Aragón, which would also contribute to a national army—it was a dream that Olivares had failed to realize the previous century.

The Council of Castilla continued to be the key legislative body in Spain, but it was developed to include departmental secretaries covering the state, justice, treasury, the Indies, and military affairs. Each province was appointed a governor along with an *intendente*, a royal official whose job included a wide range of administrative responsibilities.

During Felipe V's reign, Spain managed to regain some of the Italian territories that it had surrendered several years earlier. The driving force behind Felipe V's foreign policy was his Italian wife, Elisabeth Farnese of Parma, whose ambitions for their children had led to Spanish intervention in Italy. Following a series of conflicts and negotiations, Elisabeth and Felipe V's son Carlos was proclaimed king of Naples and Sicily in 1735.

Felipe V was not a happy man. He began to experience debilitating bouts of severe "melancholy," displaying symptoms of what today we might call manic depression. At times his behavior verged on madness, and Elisabeth Farnese gradually began to take on a greater role in matters of the Crown. In 1724, feeling he was no longer capable of ruling the country well, he announced his abdication in favor of his eldest son, seventeen-year-old Louis I, saying: "Thank god I am a king no more and that for the rest of my life I shall be at the service of God and solitude." His wishes were short-lived. Within seven months, his son was dead—struck down by smallpox. Felipe V had to be lured out of his melancholy to become king once again.

Throughout the rest of his life, the king was dogged by mental illness, which at times was so severe that, bedridden, unshaven, and unwilling to even change his clothes, he was no longer in a position to rule the country. This responsibility was left to his wife.

## Fernando VI and Carlos III

The unhappy Felipe V died in in 1746 and was succeeded by his son Fernando VI. Unfortunately, the new king suffered from the same mental affliction as his father. He had little desire to govern the country—indeed his psychological condition deteriorated to the point that he was forbidden to make public appearances or meet foreign dignitaries. The task of ruling the country was left to his ministers, who successfully steered a course of neutrality and kept the country out of further wars in Europe. With this new-found peace, unusual for Spain, the king's ministers were able to focus inwardly and continue the major Bourbon reforms throughout the realm.

Fernando VI, like his father, died in the grip of profound melancholy and mania. He was succeeded by his half-brother, Carlos III, in 1759. Unlike his predecessor, Carlos III had come to the throne already experienced in matters of government as a result of his many years as King of Naples, a position he had given up in order to take the Spanish Crown. The most enlightened of the 18th-century Bourbons, he took an active interest in the running of the country, although he relied heavily on his team of extremely able and liberal ministers.

On his arrival to the capital Madrid, Carlos III was shocked to find the city in such a run-down, dingy, and squalid condition. Determined to change this, he embarked on a series of reforms aimed at improving and instilling pride in the city—including paving the streets, constructing new buildings, and keeping the streets free of rubbish. Yet despite his interest in the capital, it was here that Carlos III would face the wrath of his subjects in the riots of 1766, which took place against a background of economic hardship and dissatisfaction over the non-Spanish ministers that he had brought with him.

Carlos III's prime minister, the Italian Marquis of Esquilache, was the man chosen to take on the unenviable task of increasing tax revenues, and in the process made himself extremely unpopular with the nobility and clergy. The reforms came at a bad time, as the country was hit by bad harvests, food shortages, and an accompanying sharp rise in the price of basic staples such as bread. Things came to a head when Esquilache introduced the seemingly bizarre law aimed at changing two important items of national dress—long loose capes and wide-brimmed hats. These articles, highly popular at the time, were singled out in the war against crime, since they hid the features of criminals, making it almost impossible to identify them, and facilitated their escape. A royal decree was issued, and from now on the length of capes and width of hats had to be reduced. Anyone not complying could find themselves stopped in the streets and set upon by eager law enforcers armed with huge scissors to cut the offending articles down to the permitted size. It was the final straw. In Madrid rioting broke out and the people demanded Esquilache's dismissal, along with the other foreigners the king had chosen as his ministers. Soon riots erupted in other cities. An angry population called for a reduction in the price of staple foods. Carlos III, who had been sufficiently worried to feel it wise to flee the capital, responded by sacking the Italian Esquilache and forming a new government—this time with Spanish ministers.

Reeling from such an attack on the Crown, Carlos III needed a scapegoat. Two groups, known to be hostile to reforms, were accused of stirring up trouble: certain factions of the nobility and the Jesuits. It was the latter who were to face the brunt of the king's displeasure. The Jesuits—priests belonging to the Catholic organization, the Society of Jesus, founded by the Spanish ex-soldier San Ignacio de Loyola (Saint Ignatious Loyola) in 1534—were a highly independent and powerful force in Spain. They were especially active in educational institutions and had their own colleges throughout the country. Yet their loyalty was first and foremost to the Pope in Rome, and not to the Spanish Monarchy. They were also openly opposed to the government's reforms. Carlos III, encouraged by one of his key ministers, José Moñino, Count of Floridablanca, took the opportunity to rid the country of them altogether. Blamed for encouraging the populace to challenge the authority of the Crown and inciting them to riot, the Jesuits were ordered to leave Spain in 1767.

Despite the riots of 1766, Carlos III's reign was to prove fruitful and was notable for its openness to the ideas of the Enlightenment. Under Carlos III's patronage, the arts and sciences flourished and royal academies were created. Universities, for so long dominated by the clergy and in a state of stagnation, were thrown open to new currents of Enlightened thought as the study of sciences was introduced. Some of the finest examples of neoclassical architecture were constructed during this period, such as the Palacio Real (Royal Palace) in Madrid, the Prado Museum, and the Puerta de Alcalá. The king's ministers

The Palacio Real de Madrid, a fine example of Spanish neoclassical architecture, built during the enlightened reign of Carlos III.

spearheaded reforms in other areas, including administration, taxation, and trade. It was also a period that saw the creation of the first national bank.

## Carlos IV

If Carlos III was generally remembered as a popular king—and the most enlightened of the Bourbons—his son Carlos IV, who succeeded him upon his death in 1788, was the opposite. His was a reign of decadence in which the gains made under his father were permitted to backslide. Before long, he was presiding over nothing short of chaos. He showed little regard for the responsibilities of his position, and lived under the domination of his wife. It was unfortunate for Spain that his reign coincided with a landmark event in European history that was to have a profound impact on the country—the French Revolution.

Within a year of Carlos IV's coronation, the violent and bloody revolution erupted in neighboring France, bringing about an air of panic in Spain. Traditional forces in the country, headed by the Church, were quick to denounce the evils of liberal ideas that had arrived with the Enlightenment. The king's minister, Floridablanca, who had been a key player in the reforms enacted of Carlos III's rule and had been kept on by Carlos IV, made a volte-face and began to enact repressive measures, including heavy press censorship, in a bid to stem the tide of liberalism. Then, in 1792, an astonishing event took place. Floridablanca was dismissed, and shortly after, a 25-year-old soldier by the name of Manuel Godoy took the job as prime minister of Spain. The young Godoy, who was known for his good looks, owed his extraordinary rise through the ranks to the king's wife, who had taken a fancy to him.

Meanwhile, events in France moved rapidly. In the same year of 1792, the French King Louis XVI was arrested and tried for treason; the monarchy was abolished; and the country was declared a Republic. The following year, in a chilling and bloody final act of regicide, Louis XVI and his queen Marie Antoinette were sent to the guillotine. The executions profoundly shocked the European monarchies. In response, they closed ranks to form an alliance against the French. Godoy, who had now taken full command of the Spanish army, made the decision to join them, underestimating the strength of the new French regime. Before long, French troops were occupying towns in Catalonia and the Basque country, and looked set to push further into Spanish territory. In 1795, desperate to get the French out, Spain signed a treaty with the new Republic. As part of the deal, the Spanish were forced to surrender their part of the Caribbean island of Santo Domingo. Godoy had led the country into a humiliating defeat; yet in a rather bewildering gesture, Carlos VI promptly awarded him the highest honor of *Príncipe de la Paz* (Prince of Peace).

Manuel Godoy.

# The Napoleonic Wars

In a subsequent about-face, Godoy now joined forces with the French against Britain and Portugal and embarked on a series of disastrous battles. In 1797, the Spanish navy faced a humiliating defeat at the hands of the British off the southern coast of Portugal, at the Battle of Cape St. Vincente. To avoid further trouble, Spain surrendered the Caribbean island of Trinidad to the British in the Peace of Amiens in 1802. Despite a short respite, it was not long before the Spanish navy was once again headed on a collision course with the British.

In Europe, Napoleon Bonaparte's star had been rising for several years. After staging a successful coup in 1799, he had assumed the leadership of the French Republic and set about carving out a vast European empire, proclaiming himself emperor in 1804. He was a brilliant general who, until his downfall in 1813, achieved outstanding results in the battlefield against the European coalitions that united against him.

Yet not all of his campaigns were successful. As part of his plan to attack Britain by landing an army of 160,000 men on its soil, Napoleon promised Godoy handsome rewards if he would put the Spanish navy at the service of the French. No sooner said than done, the huge combined

Napolean meeting Carlos IV

Spanish and French fleet was confronted by the British navy in 1805 at the Battle of Trafalgar, which took place just off the coast of Cádiz in southern Spain. Headed by the British admiral Lord Nelson who was fated to die in the conflict, the British left their enemies' fleets in utter ruins. It was a devasting blow for Spain, which had once again lost

Admiral Lord Nelson lies mortally wounded at the
Battle of Trafalgar.

its naval power to the English—a vital force in the protection of its
American colonies.

Napoleon was determined to bring Britain to heel. If a swift military
victory was out of the question, then he would try to devastate the
British economy by cutting it off from its vital European markets by
means of a blockade. To ensure its success, he first needed to deal with
the Portuguese, who had defied the French and continued trading with
their British ally. To this end, Napoleon proposed to launch a joint
French-Spanish attack on Portugal. An agreement was reached with
Spain whereby French troops would be granted access across its
territory to the Portuguese border. However, Napoleon soon began
stationing his troops in Spanish towns that had nothing to do with the
Portuguese campaign.

Meanwhile, Carlos IV, and his son, Prince Fernando, had fallen out
with each other. Their relationship degenerated to such a point that

Fernando, who been plotting to depose his father, ended up being thrown in prison. There was worse to follow. The king and his incompetent minister Godoy were in no doubt as to their unpopularity after riots broke out in Aranjuez outside the royal palace. Carlos VI had no alternative but to dismiss his thoroughly detested minister, and several days later he himself abdicated in favor of his son, Fernando VII.

What was already a fiasco turned into an outrageous farce. Carlos VI and Fernando VII began to vie for Napoleon's attention—in short, Carlos wanted his throne back and Fernando wanted to keep it. Napoleon ordered father and son, whom he later referred to as "imbeciles," to Bayonne in southern France to sort out their problems. With French troops now in Spain, having been invited in to attack Portugal, and the Spanish royal family effectively prisoners in France, Napoleon quite simply took over Spain. Carlos and Fernando were made to renounce their rights to the throne; and Napoleon proclaimed his own brother, Joseph Bonaparte, king of Spain.

The turn of events caused outrage throughout Spain. Few were prepared to stand idly by while Napoleon plotted the future of their country.

## The War of Independence

Joseph Bonaparte, known in Spain as José I, was proclaimed king in 1808. A minority welcomed him—some hoped for a return to the enlightened monarchy exemplified by Carlos III, while others were merely opportunists. Most Spaniards, however, rejected him outright, believing his rule to be entirely without legitimacy. From the beginning, José I, known as *Pepe Botellas* ("Joe Bottles") on account of his well-known drinking habits, found himself in the midst of a major popular rebellion. This insurrection marked the beginning of a five-year struggle to expel the French invaders from the country, which became known as the War of Independence.

The first serious trouble was in Madrid. On May 2, 1808, shortly before José I was proclaimed king, the city's inhabitants rose up in arms

The highly unpopular Godoy surrounded by Spanish soldiers after being seized during the Aranjuez riots of 1808.

against the new invaders; yet the French were quick to quash the revolt. The punishment was swift and merciless. The following day, French firing squads busied themselves shedding the blood of the citizens of Madrid. The terror was immortalized by the famous contemporary Spanish painter Francisco Goya, whose depictions of the conflict now hang in the Prado Museum in Madrid.

Juntas began to spring up in each region, swearing loyalty to Fernando VII. Those who supported José I were set upon by angry mobs. The situation was explosive and the whole country was soon plunged into a war against France, which was notorious for its ferocity and cruelty. In July 1808, the Spanish managed to defeat a French force that had entrenched itself in the south. Elsewhere they put up a spirited resistance.

In order to control the rapidly deteriorating situation, Napoleon marched an army of some 300,000 men over the border into Spain. Far

The Prado Museum, built by Carlos III, which today houses many of Goya's
masterpieces, along with many other famous works of art.

outnumbered, there was no way the disorganized Spanish armies, in
which peasants and regular troops fought alongside each other, could
meet the French army face to face. The conflict instead took on the
nature of guerilla warfare. *Guerrilleros*, who relied on the support of the
people, moved around in small groups attacking and ambushing
Napoleon's forces and, little by little, wearing them down. In a new
twist, the Spanish had now found themselves a new ally—France's
worst enemy, Britain, which was to prove a most useful partner.

## Spanish Liberalism and the 1812 Constitution

In an attempt to keep some form of national government in operation
during the war, a central junta for Spain and its colonies, known as the
*Junta Central Suprema*, was organized. After a period in Sevilla, the
junta was moved further south to Cádiz to escape the onslaught of the
French. In the besieged Andalusian port of Cádiz, protected by Spanish
troops and the guns of the British navy (which only a few years earlier

devasted Spain's own fleet at the Battle of Trafalgar off the same stretch of coast), the leaders of the *Junta Central Suprema* set about drafting a new national constitution.

To this end, there was a summoning of the Cortes, the Spanish term for parliament. Delegates from all the provinces were sent for, though with the country at war many were not able to attend. These, as well as delegates for the American colonies, were subsituted by representives chosen from the population of Cádiz, whose influential middle classes were extremely open to progressive ideas and inspired by the French Revolution. These men subsequently became known as "liberals," a political term first used in Spain.

The fruit of their labor was the Constitution of 1812, which challenged the very basis of the traditional and conservative forces of the country. In a dramatic move, it declared that sovereignty lay in the

Troops of the French Army—both ally and enemy in the stormy French-Spanish relations during the late 18th and early 19th centuries.

nation and not the king. It was a rejection of the absolutism of the Bourbon monarchy that many considered responsible for leading Spain down the road to ruin. From now on, the king would have limited powers and be subject to parliament. Men were given the right to vote; and there was to be a single-chamber parliament to which deputies from around the country would be elected. The privileges enjoyed by the aristocracy, which for so long had kept the countryside in a state of near feudalism, were abolished. Individual rights such as freedom of speech and association were upheld and, although the Church was to remain the state religion, the Inquisition was abolished.

In short, Spain's first attempt at a constitutional monarchy aimed to do no less than pull down the traditional structures of power. In its place was to be a system of government that displayed some of the key characteristics to be found in a modern democratic state. At that time, only one other country in the world had a written constitution—the United States. Yet, the fact that the constitution was so radical reflected the absence of representation of many of the country's traditional forces, such as the nobility and the Church, who would never have countenanced such liberties. It was not long before these two groups were rallying behind the monarchy and challenging the liberals.

The same year, the War of Independence took a new turn. Britain marched an army of some 50,000 men into Spain under the leadership of the Duke of Wellington and defeated Napoleon's troops in Salamanca. The following year, joint Spanish, Portuguese, and British forces had the French in full retreat. After being soundly defeated in Vitoria, José I finally threw in the towel and fled the country in 1814. The War of Independence had come to an end.

## The Restoration of the Bourbon Monarchy

Despite his lamentable reputation, Fernando VII was welcomed back to Spain in triumph, amidst a wave of popular support. He had already proven himself to be a highly disreputable character; and during his reign he would certainly live up to this reputation, helping to draw Spain into what was certainly one of the grimmest periods in its history.

The country that he returned to was profoundly divided. On one side there were the liberals, those who saw Spain's future tied to the 1812 Constitution of Cádiz; and on the other were those who welcomed with open arms a return to the old days. Heartily encouraged by his supporters, Fernando VII abolished the constitution and set about reviving the old institutions that had been the pillars of absolutism. He purged the government of liberals and other undesirables, such as those who had supported José I, and surrounded himself with stalwarts of the old regime. The constitution was abolished and the Inquisition reinstated. But the radical ideas that had inspired the 1812 Constitution were still alive in Spain and could not be

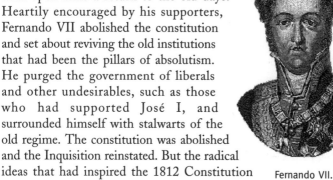

Fernando VII.

eradicated. The genie had been let out of the bottle and, for many years to come, the traditional conservative forces—strongest amongst the aristocracy and clergy—were to attempt the impossible and force it back in.

## The Independence of Latin America

Napoleon's conquest of Spain spelled the beginning of the end of Spain's American colonies. The upheaval in the mother country had thrown them into a state of confusion. Without the legitimate monarch on the throne, where did the loyalty of the Spanish Indies lie?

Whatever the case, it was certainly not to José I. Cut off from Spain, the colonies began to lose direction. Political divisions and resentments between the *criollos* (those Spaniards born in the Americas) and the Spanish government, which had been brewing for some time, came erupting to the surface. With the promise of greater representation in the Indies afforded by the Cádiz Constitution of 1812, the *criollo*-dominated middle-class took the opportunity to push for a degree of autonomy. They wanted, amongst other things, an end to the monopoly that prevented them from trading with foreigners and an equal chance to compete for government posts, which the state preferred to reserve for those born in Spain.

Yet few in Spain were prepared to upset the system that had for so long boosted the coffers of the state through taxes and duties and had generated handsome profits for Spanish merchants—the very same class who had played a pivotal role in the liberal Constitution. Little progress was made as representatives of all sides argued over the future governance of the Americas. Meanwhile the viceroys of the Indies, who were staunch defenders of the old system, did all they could to thwart the introduction of liberal freedoms guaranteed by the constitution.

Some of the more radical elements were not prepared to negotiate with the Spanish authorities at all. For them, the answer was no less than full independence from Spain. With Spain still in turmoil and unable to impose order, armed independence movements spread like wildfire throughout the Indies. In Mexico, the *criollo* priest, Miguel Hidalgo, led an uprising against the Spanish on September 16, 1810. In Venezuela, Simón de Bolivar and Francisco de Miranda declared a new independent republic on July 5, 1811. Elsewhere, rebellions threatened to bring down the established order that for three centuries had held sway over the Spanish Indies.

Once the Bourbon monarchy was re-established, Spain was eager to focus its attention on the rebellious colonies. Fernando VII would countenance nothing less than the full restoration of royal authority. Although royalist forces succeeded in regaining control in Mexico and Venezuela, it would need a serious commitment of Spanish forces to fully restore order in the Indies. Yet the country was in financial and economic ruins; and its army was thoroughly demoralized, languishing in a state of neglect.

Over the next few years, the independence movements gathered fresh momentum. In 1820, determined to put an end to rebellion, the government assembled an special expeditionary force. But its officers had no motivation to fight for a regime that had treated the army with such little respect; and their men had even less desire to face death in an unknown land far away from home. As the troops bound for the Americas were waiting to embark ships in the port of Cádiz, a group of officers led a mutiny against the government. Taking control of the expeditionary force, they marched on Madrid and demanded the restoration of the 1812 Constitution. They pointed the finger of blame for country's sorrowful condition squarely at Fernando's VII's corrupt government—a sentiment shared by many other military officers. The king had no option but to accept their terms.

The independence movements were quick to take advantage of the chaos. The fight for independence was now in full swing. The royal forces could do nothing as, one by one, the new Latin American republics sprang up, declaring independence from Spain. By 1830, Spain's American colonies had been reduced to just two islands, Cuba and Puerto Rico. Centuries of Spanish domination in the region had come to an end.

# The Return of the Liberals

Meanwhile, in the Spanish peninsular, the liberals were now back in power, and the process of liberal reform began again. The gains made by the traditionalists during the last few years were reversed. However, divisions between the liberals soon began to appear. They splintered into two groups known as *exaltados* and *moderados*. The *moderados* were, as their name suggests, the moderate liberals who were worried that the constitution encompassed ideas that were too radical and dangerous for the country, and who argued in favor of a less far-reaching constitution. This idea was met with disgust by the *exaltados*, the radical liberals, who were keen to see the whole program of constitutional reforms, and more, carried out.

Catalan men and women wearing traditional 19th-century clothes found in the region—the man holding the staff with the cross is a Jesuit official.

They did not have long to wait. Winning elections held in 1822, the *exaltados* took control of the government. The country was plunged into crisis. Civil unrest spread throughout the country in response to the new government's proposed economic reforms and to its hostile treatment of the Church. The peasants themselves rallied behind anti-government movements in protest of the government's aim to do away with common pastures and bring them under private ownership.

In the confusion that followed, troops proclaiming their loyalty to the king attempted to overthrow the government in Madrid. They were soon defeated, and instead a new and ever more radical government was formed. Other European powers, with little desire to see a disruption of the balance of power, had been following events in Spain closely. As the situation deteriorated, France, with the blessing of its allies in Europe, marched an army into Spain in order to bring an end to the liberal experiment and rescue the absolute monarchy of Fernando VII.

Wholesale purging of liberals from government posts and the army began again in earnest. The Church, which enjoyed widespread support around the country, voiced its disapproval of liberal ideas louder than ever. Under Fernando VII's rule, the country once more limped on, with his ministers desperately attempting to revive the country's ailing economy. Meanwhile, the opposition forces in the country were becoming more extreme; and it seemed that the next crisis was not far off.

## The Carlist Wars

Fernando VII was heading towards the same kind of royal trouble that had plagued many of Spain's monarchs—that of succession. Under an 18th-century law, women were prohibited from ascending to the throne; thus Fernando VII's daughter, Isabel, was ineligible as an heir. This fact left the king in a tricky position. Realizing that he was unlikely to have a son, the king opted to simply change the law. It gave a group of extreme royalists, who were rabidly anti-liberal and unimpressed by Fernando VII's government, a perfect excuse to make trouble. For some years they had been identifying themselves more and more with the king's brother, Carlos. Soon other traditional forces, including the clergy, also warmed to the idea of having him as king—and it was a role Carlos himself was only too happy to assume.

When Fernando VII died in 1833, Carlos promptly declared himself king. In the meantime, Fernando VII's supporters proclaimed three-year–old Isabel as the rightful monarch and her mother María Cristina as daughter regent. Divided over the fundamental issue of succession, Spain had a serious problem on its hands. Civil war loomed large on the horizon.

Carlos's supporters, known as the *carlistas*, were mainly concentrated in the north of Spain, in regions such as Navarra, the Basque Country, and parts of Aragón and Catalonia. These were areas that had traditionally enjoyed special privileges from the Crown and where the Church enjoyed a great deal of popularity. As the *carlistas* rallied behind their favorite, Isabel's regent-mother set about trying to gain the desperately needed support of the moderate liberals by offering them concessions.

To this end, María Cristina chose a *moderado*, Francisco Martínez de la Rosa, as chief minister. Martínez de la Rosa set about drafting a Royal Statute that provided for a parliament with an upper and lower house. The first was for nobles and important members of the clergy, and the second was for deputies who were elected from an extremely restricted electorate. It was not nearly enough to satisfy the liberals and many, especially those more radically inclined, demanded more. María Cristina bowed to political pressure, and appointed a new minister, Juan Álvarez Mendizábal, to oversee further reforms.

Mendizábal's key problem was how to find money to pay for the war to put an end to Carlist designs. His solution was one relished by the *exaltados*—the selling-off of church and communal lands. It was a decision that, although accepted by many at the time as a necessary measure, was to sow the bitter seeds of discontent. The Church would never forgive the liberals for inflicting such a blow. Mendizábal was the latest in the line of Spanish liberals who had attempted to cut the lands free from the ancient laws and to open them up to market forces. They wanted laws introduced that would permit the right to buy and sell land and contract labor freely. In their line of fire was the centuries-old feudal-like system, which still remained rooted in the countryside.

Meanwhile, Spain was in the midst of a conflict that became known as the First Carlist War. During the early stages, forces loyal to Isabel II fared badly. In 1837, the *carlistas* came close to taking Madrid. Yet their fate changed as the army, ultimately better organized and equipped, thanks to Medizábal's efforts at securing British backing, gained the upper hand. In 1839, the *carlistas* were forced to recognize Isabel II and accept a peace deal negotiated by General Baldomero Espartero, a man who was to dominate Spanish politics for the foreseeable future.

With the victory, Isabel II had emerged in a stronger position, but the clear winner was Espartero, who rose to become head of government and took over as regent. Isabel's mother was forced into exile in France. The Carlist problem was temporarily dealt with, but it would not entirely go away. It lay festering only to erupt, six years later, into a second war. This time the *carlistas* rose against the queen on behalf of Carlos's heir. Once again though, they met with defeat.

# Isabel II

Isabel II finally came to power, in 1843, at the tender age of thirteen. The decision to put such a young queen on the throne was taken in order to avoid replacing Espartero, who by now had fallen from grace, with yet another regent. Isabel II was thrown into the volatile world of Spanish politics, which was characterized by seemingly endless changes of government and civil war. The fact that during the next decade of her reign the country enjoyed enough stability to allow the realization of many liberal reforms was not due to Isabel II. She showed little flair for government, and was generally an unpopular monarch whose reign became tarnished by corruption. Furthermore, she scandalized the

19th-century Galician peasants performing a dance, accompanied by drum, castanets, and a tambourine. The man on the left is playing a tradional Galician instrument, similar to bagpipes.

19th-century inhabitants of Mallorca, one of the Spanish Balearic Islands.

nation by taking on a host of different lovers—although this was tempered by the widely known revelation that she was in a desperately unhappy marriage to a man who had married her out of a sense of duty and who, by all accounts, could scarcely tolerate her presence.

The leadership of her government passed onto a *moderado* by the name of Ramón María Narváez. Despite various set-backs, his liberal government performed the remarkable feat of lasting ten years, between 1844 and 1854. During this breathing space, liberalism found fertile ground in which to thrive. It was not the kind of radical liberalism that had presented such a challenge to the established order, but a more moderate kind characterized by constitutionalism and a restricted citizen's bill of rights. Narváez's government not only enjoyed widespread support amongst the middle classes but also that of a good section of the upper classes. It drew up a new constitution in which national sovereignty was based in the Crown and the Cortes. The Cortes was comprised of the Senate, whose members were to be chosen by Isabel II, as well as the Congress, whose deputies were to be elected by slightly more than one percent of the population.

Spain found itself undergoing an economic revival. It was also during this period that work began on Spain's first railway lines. The first was built between Barcelona and Mataró in Catalonia in 1848; and another line constructed between the capital Madrid and Albacete, to the southeast, was completed by 1855. Other public works included the construction of major roads and the improvement of ports. It was also a time which saw the birth of the peseta (the national currency), as well as the introduction of a paid postage system (1849) and the telegraph (1852). Another notable achievement was the establishment of primary schools.

In the early 1850s, the government found itself rocked by a series of financial scandals and faced serious accusations of corruption. Unable to limit the damage or give a convincing account of itself, it faced ever angrier opposition and civil unrest. Isabella II was also proving to be highly unpopular. She showed a tendency to interfere in matters of the state by hiring and firing ministers at will and frustrating any real sense of continuity in the reform of the country. In what was to become almost a Spanish tradition, there was a military revolt against the government—known as a *pronunciamiento* in Spanish—not far from the capital. The situation was highly volatile and was accompanied by anti-government riots in Madrid and other Spanish cities. With events slipping out of control, Isabel II called her one-time chief minister, Espartero, to restore order.

A new government was established, headed by Espartero himself. Under his leadership, the government launched into a program of further liberal reforms. But Isabella II got cold feet over her new minister's progressive policies and replaced him with more moderate prime ministers. For the next few years Spain enjoyed a period of relative economic growth and stability. The country's pride in the international arena, for so long seriously dented, also received a little boost as its forces pursued various successful foreign military campaigns in South America, and aided the French in their bid to colonize Vietnam. In Morocco there were significant gains as the army took control of Tetuán, in northern Morocco.

The respite was not long lived. When a new economic crisis hit the country in the mid-1860s, there were waves of unrest throughout the country. The government came under a barrage of sustained criticism from the progressive liberals, and the soon the situation deteriorated to such an extent that revolution was once again in the air. In 1868, the army did not disappoint and issued a *pronuciamiento*, supported by the progressive liberal oppostition parties. The coup was led by an admiral, Juan Topete, and two progressive generals—Juan Prim y Prats and Francisco Serrano (incidentally, Isabella's ex-lover). Defeating the queen's troops, Prim y Prats and Serrano marched into Madrid to a tumultuous reception proclaiming the end of the Bourbon dynasty. The by now "intolerable" Isabel II, no longer welcome in Spain, was forced to flee to France.

## Six Revolutionary Years

With Isabel II gone, Spain was now without a monarch. For six revolutionary years, the country would stagger desperately from one political system to another, with no less than thirteen changes of leadership as it struggled to find a viable form of government.

Having successfully defeated the government forces after the 1868 *pronunciamiento*, the victorious generals set about forming a provisional government, headed by Serrano. Elections were held in which the liberal Progressive Party won a majority. A new constitution was drawn up and accepted in 1869, declaring Spain a constitutional monarchy and guaranteeing, along with the vote, a host of other civil rights. Still, a new monarch, who was not a Bourbon, had to be found. But from where?

One solution was attempted by General Prim y Prats who, in the absence of the queen, had assumed the role of regent. After searching throughout Europe for a monarch, Prim y Prats thought he had found a suitable candidate in the Amadeo of Savoy, the son of the King of Italy. In November 1870, the Cortes elected him Amadeo I of Spain. Yet the unfortunate king was doomed from the beginning. The following month, his mentor Prim y Prats was assassinated in Madrid, leaving the new monarch to face the chaos of Spanish politics. It was asking the impossible. The initial elation of bringing down Isabel II's regime had worn off and and now whatever common sense of purpose that might have existed amongst the parties had degenerated into bitter feuding. Added to this was a resurgence of the belligerent *carlistas* who were stirring up trouble in Navarra and the Catalonian countryside. Enough was enough. Amadeo I, who had shown himself to be a reasonable and diplomatic enough monarch, threw in the towel and abdicated in 1873.

Having ousted the existing Bourbon monarchy and chased away the new replacement, Spain was drifting into increasingly dangerous waters as it struggled on without a head of state. The question now was who could do the job. It was time for the Republicans to try their hand at government. In February 1873, in a radical move, the Cortes declared Spain to be a republic. It lasted no longer than eleven months, during which time there were no less than four presidents. Its key failure lay in its ability to control forces in the country who were opposed to a strong, or indeed any, central government.

Bowing to pressure from the federalists who were demanding autonomy for the various regions in Spain, a new constitution was created that divided the country in fifteen states. It proved to be a can of worms. Soon states were declaring themselves to be republics, and within the republics, revolutionary groups were even declaring cities themselves to be independent. Added to this, the *carlistas* were now in full-scale revolt and, across the Atlantic, revolution broke out the Spanish colony of Cuba. Spain appeared to be disintegrating, its unity shaken to the core. It was time for the generals to step in once again. In January 1874, there was another *pronuciamiento,* and the military assumed control of the country.

The situation was desperate. Since the queen had been deposed, nothing had gone right. There seemed only one solution—to re-establish the Bourbons. Queen Isabella II, still in exile, was persuaded to step aside and allow her son to become the king of Spain. It was a solution that met with the general approval of the army; and in December 1874, the army proclaimed Alfonso XII the new king of Spain. The seventeen-year-old Alfonso, fresh out of the prestigious military academy of Sandhurst in England, arrived in Spain the following month.

## Benito Pérez Galdós—A Chronicler of his Time

The upheavals of the period greatly influence the work of Benito Pérez Galdós, regarded by many to be the greatest Spanish novelist after Cervantes. While he was born in the Canary Islands in 1843, he was to spend most of his life in Madrid. Galdós was a liberal-minded writer whose religious scepticism earned him a reputation for being anticlerical. Yet, his writing was full of psychological insight and suffused with Christian idealism.

Through his novels he chronicled the social and political upheavals that were taking place during the 19th century and the tensions between the new-found liberalism and traditional society in Spain. His novel, *Doña Perfecta*, written in 1876, demonstrated his somewhat pessimistic outlook on life in the conservative Spanish countryside of his day.

The work tells of the story of the clash between Pepe, a liberal-minded and tolerant man, and Doña Perfecta, a fanatical Catholic and *carlista*, who will stop at nothing to prevent Pepe from marrying her daughter, Rosario. As the drama unfolds, Doña Perfecta, goaded by her priest and confessor, embarks on ruthless and hypocritical campaign of hate against Pepe, resulting in his tragic death and in Rosario being sent to a lunatic asylum. Galdós's novel, as it sets the two sides against each other, is a skilfully crafted commentary of the time, and demonstrates his concern over the loss of the liberal gains made by the 1868 Revolution as a result of the restoration of the Bourbon monarchy.

Galdós threw his whole life into his work, so much so that, by the time of his death in 1920, he had written no less than 77 novels.

# Cánovas and the System of Alternating Governments

In 1876, with the Bourbon monarch now restored, Spain once again adopted a new constitution. There was no reason to believe that this would be any more successful than its predecessors—the latest in a long line of failed attempts to impose law and order on what had now become a wild and unruly country. Yet, surprisingly, it proved to be durable and, despite gradually running into serious problems, it was to remain in effect until 1923.

The constitution was the brainchild of the conservative politician and new prime minister, Antonio Cánovas del Castillo. With the threat of social revolution hanging over the country, the urgent problem that Cánovas faced was how to establish a regime that was acceptable to the most influential forces of the country. He also sought to find a way to prevent a repetition of the by now chronic tendency of the military to intervene in politics with their all too frequent *pronuciamentos*.

Studying the previous constitutions, Cánovas salvaged the elements that seemed to be the most appropriate for the country and would satisfy as many people as possible. To Cánovas's thinking, there was no doubt that the monarchy, which had been such an integral part of the nation for centuries, had to stay. This was an opinion shared by a great many, not least by the army. Therefore, a republic was out of the question. Furthermore, since the Catholic Church played a fundamental part in the identity of Spain, Cánovas felt it was vital to allow it to continue its role as the state religion, although he allowed for the freedom to practice other faiths.

Antonio Cánovas, one of Spain's most influential politicians of the 19th century.

Cánovas had to entice the both the conservatives, to whom he belonged, and the liberals into accepting the new constitution. In exchange for their support, he would guarantee them a role in the governing of the country. The result was what amounted to a remarkable agreement between the politicians and the king to frequently alternate two governments, always conservative and liberal, in response to the various political and economic crises that developed. The decision to change the government was made by the politicians and sanctioned by the king, who would then dissolve the Cortes. Therefore, the conservatives would govern for a period of time; and when things got to difficult for them, the liberals would take over until they too ran into problems. It was aptly named the *turno pacífico*, meaning the "peaceful rotation." The change of government would make people feel that the problems were being addressed.

In order to give the impression that the governments were elected by the public, a system of practically total electoral manipulation was established. Changing from a liberal to a conservative government, or vice versa, meant finding the required number of votes and this was not an easy task to pull off—especially after voting rights were extended to all men in 1890. To this end, a system called *caciquismo*, which relied on men called *caciques*, developed to ensure that the chosen party won at the elections. *Cacique* was taken from an American Indian word meaning a "village chief." The Spanish government depended on these local bosses to use their influence to deliver the votes. *Caciques* would promise favors such as tax or military service exemptions in exchange for political support, as well as resorting to a whole range of other fraudulent and underhanded practices.

Of course the government could not be seen to publicly condone such behavior, yet it was an integral part of the system. Some highly imaginitive ways were soon dreamed up to ensure that the right political candidates were elected. As well as straightforward harassment or even the arrest of voters, the times and places of voting were changed with such short notice that only those voting favorably could participate. Other tricks might be locating voting stations in unfavorable or unsavory locations to discourage voters—such as in a hospital with a raging epidemic. It was not even uncommon for the village dead to cast their votes—a miracle made possible by including the names of the deceased on the electoral registers and hiring gangs known as *lázaros*, after the biblical Lazarus who rose from the dead, to vote in their place.

Alfonso XII and María Cristina.

Things went fairly smoothly at first. The conservative and liberal governments were led by Cánovas and Práxedes Mateo Sagasta respectively, with Alfonso XII as king. However, the king's life was cut short by tuberculosis in 1885—he was only 28 years old. Although he had no children at the time of his untimely death, his wife, María Cristina of Hapsburg, was carrying his child. It was a delicate situation. Cánovas and Sagasta, well aware of the potential chaos that could be caused the power vacuum, immediately made a pact. In the Pacto del Pardo, it was agreed that both parties would continue to respect the system of alternating governments—in other words, when it was time to be replaced they would go peacefully and wait until it was their turn again. Moreover, they would agree to accept María Cristina as regent until her child, later named Alfonso, was old enough to take the throne. It worked, and the system held fast.

In 1897, while taking a rest at a health resort during his term as prime minister, the 69-year-old Cánovas was shot dead by an Italian anarchist. Although the system he had engineered was to survive him for many years to come, the road ahead was distinctly rocky. The very thing that made the the system work was leading it into trouble. It was a regime whose fundamental distrust of the electorate and army led it to depend on thoroughly disreputable and corrupt practices. Furthermore, the continuous alternation of governments, which were practically identical, brought little change to a country badly in need of radical reform. As a result, powerful social and political forces began to organize themselves outside a regime that chose to ignore them.

## The Loss of Cuba

The death of Cánovas coincided with a landmark event in Spanish history—the loss of Cuba, which brought Spanish colonial history to a final and humiliating end. After the independence of Latin America, Spain was now limited to a few overseas possessions including the Philippines, Puerto Rico, and Cuba. The latter, one of Spain's first colonies, had become an important sugar producer during the 19th century. The island's most important trading partner was the United States.

Cuba's plantations were dependent on slaves and as a result many landowners, fearing international pressure to abolish slavery, established closer links with their counterparts in the southern United States. Some Cubans even argued that to better protect their interests, the island should be incorporated into the United States. Yet when slavery was abolished after the American Civil War, this was no longer an option. In 1868, rebellion broke out in Cuba over the Spanish government's continued refusal to allow slave-owners a greater say in the running of the island. This insurrection escalated into an all-out war of independence against Spain, which raged on for ten years and finally ended in failure— but not before wreaking terrible havoc on the economy. The result was an even greater dependence on the United States, which had both the capital and the markets to revive the sugar industry. The Spanish government continued to ignore the question of greater autonomy in Cuba.

The desire for Cuban independence proved to be unquenchable and fighting broke out once more. With the stability of the island at stake, the USA, with its by now substantial economic as well as strategic interests in the region, was no mere impartial observer. Despite

A Spanish recruit leaves his distraught family to fight the war in Cuba.

desperate last-minute efforts by the Spanish to address the issue of autonomy, it was too late.

In 1898, the U.S. battleship *SS Maine* was destroyed in an explosion in the port of Havana, killing more than 260 of its crew. Despite the fact that no responsibility was established for the disaster, the United States declared war on the Spanish government. The result was catastrophic for Spain. The United States struck first in the Spanish colony of the Philippines, devastating its navy, and then turned its guns on the Spanish fleet in Cuba. Spain did not stand a chance and had no choice but to accept defeat. In the peace treaty that followed, the Spanish surrendered Cuba, Puerto Rico, and the Philippines to the United States. It was a bleak period in Spanish history and one which would be refered to from now on as simply *El Desastre*—"The Disaster." Spain had finally losts its overseas colonies; and in a Europe that judged the international status of a country by its colonial might, it was a humiliating defeat. The prime minister, Sagasta, under whose liberal administration "The Disaster" had happened, resigned.

There was a great deal of soul-searching in Spain as the country struggled to come to terms with its loss. It found its best expression amongst a group of writers, later known as the "generation of 98," who began to question what it meant to be Spanish and where the future of the country lay. Amongst these were two of Spain's most influential writers, Miguel de Unamuno and José Ortega y Gasset. For many of these new thinkers, there was a feeling that it was now time to make a decisive break with the past and thoroughly modernize and Europeanize the country.

## Gaudí—A Towering Architectural Genius

As Spain was undergoing a profound identity crisis, one man was busy forging a unique style of architecture that sought not to break with the past, but marry it with the modern. His name was Antoni Gaudí i Cornet, an architect who has become almost legendary in Catalonia and whose works have become a very part of the region's identity.

Gaudí was born in Reus, near Barcelona, in 1852, the son of a boilermaker. His work, mostly constructed in his native Barcelona, drew on a variety of sources including Moorish and Gothic architecture and included elements of the Arte Nouveau which was in vogue at the time. The result was a series of astonishing buildings, whose often playful quality gave them the appearance of belonging to a strange and wonderful fantasy world.

While he spent much of his youth mixing with avant-garde poets, artists and musicians, as he got older he became increasingly eccentric and reclusive as he obsessively pursued his work. Early on his career, Gaudí was fortunate to find himself a patron in the person of Count Eusebi Güell, the son of an extremely wealthy Catalan industrialist, whom he met in 1878. It proved to be a fruitful and enduring relationship, with Güell happy to allow the architect an almost free hand in the buildings he produced.

In 1900, Gaudí began work on the dream-like Parc Güell, intended as a "garden city." With panoramic views over Barcelona, the park features a fairy tale landscape of man-made and natural forms that blend together to give a unique and dream-like effect. A special feature is the use of mosaics that adorn the surfaces of the structures, made up of materials such as tiles and pieces of marble, glass, and pottery

Gaudí was an extremely religious person who believed that rightfully motivated architecture could help to redeem modern man. In keeping with his religious nature, one project was to dominate his life. This was the construction of the church of the Sagrada

Facade of the Casa Milà, Barcelona— built by Gaudí between 1905 and 1910.

Familia in Barcelona, begun in the 1880s. The huge project became such a integral part of his life that, between 1909 and his death in 1926, he devoted himself entirely to it, working and sleeping on site with little regard for the comforts of life. The building turned into a material embodiment of his highly imaginative ideas of structure and form. As the building developed so to did his ideas—which often came in the form of visions. The result is one of the most remarkable buildings in

Scenes from the dream-like gardens of Parc Güell in Barcelona—created between 1900 and 1914 by Antoni Gaudí. (Below—a close-up of a mosaic seat design.)

Building showing Gaudí's Moorish influence

the history of architecture, featuring tapering towers that soar into the sky like enormous ventilated stalagmites, crowned with crosses.

One afternoon in June 1926, while on his way to church to pray, Gaudí was fatally injured after being knocked down by a trolley bus in a major street in Barcelona. Onlookers believed the white-haired disheveled man to be a tramp and took him to a pauper's ward in hospital, where he received only rudimentary treatment and died shortly after. After realizing their mistake, the citizens of Barcelona atoned by giving him a grand funeral. Fittingly his body is buried in the crypt of the Sagrada Familia.

Gaudí in fact never lived to see the completion of his most cherished project, and work on the highly original and striking church is still in progress today. Gaudí himself is still held with such esteem in Catalonia that, in 1998, the cardinal of Barcelona nominated him for sainthood on account of his "profound and constant contemplation of the mysteries of faith."

## Alfonso XIII—A Reign of Crisis

Spain began the 20th century amidst growing disillusionment on the part of the people with its government. With the new century also came a new king as Alfonso XIII, Alfonso XII's posthumous son, came of age in 1902. There was a gradual weakening of control over events in the country on the part of the liberal and conservative parties, which continued to take turns governing the country. Although reformists on both sides of Canovas's alternating party system emerged who recognized the need to reform the regime and get rid of the corrupt practice of *caciquismo*, nothing fundamentally changed. The system was growing unstable as prime ministers were changed with alarming frequency in response to various troubles that beset the country.

In 1909, events came to a head in Barcelona when violence erupted, sparked off by the government's decision to send Catalan army reservists to fight a war in Morocco. The protest initially took the form of a general strike, but gradually escalated into major riots, in which a whole range of groups vented their rage and frustration against the regime. Known as the *Semana Trágica*, meaning the "Tragic Week," scores of protesters were killed in bloody confrontations with government troops. In the midst of the chaos, the clergy also faced the wrath of angry groups, and many churches and monasteries were desecrated, looted, or burned. In the aftermath of the carnage, an anarchist by the name of Francisco Ferrer y Guardia was made into a scapegoat, sentenced to death, and promptly taken out and shot before a firing squad. The case caused an enormous national and international outcry. The conservative prime minister, Antonio Maura, was forced to resign over his handling of the affair. In keeping with the system, the liberals then took over power.

The *Semana Trágica* was a clear sign that the system was breaking down. Politicians were losing control of the country and found it increasingly difficult to quell the malaise in their own ranks. Maura's resignation over his management of the crisis, and his subsequent refusal to participate in the *turno pácifico*, left King Alfonso XIII presiding over a regime that was incapable of presenting him with viable governments. Between 1910 and 1923, there were no less than fifteen different governments.

A real cause for concern was the rise of the Anarchist and Socialist movements, which had steadily been growing in popularity since their introduction in the latter part of the previous century. With them came the powerful weapon of the working class: the strike. Large numbers of dissatisfied workers were channeled into organized labor movements. These flourished and grew outside the system that had failed to represent them.

Two key workers' movements were to play a major role in the historical events of the next few decades that led up to the tragic Spanish Civil War: the General Union of Workers (UGT) founded in 1888, and the National Confederation of Workers (CNT) founded in 1910. The UGT, a socialist union, was the more moderate of the two. The CNT, on the other hand, was an enormous anarchist movement that was dedicated to nothing less than overthrowing the state. The CNT's belligerent posture was to lead to serious confrontations with the government, which, ever reliant on the army, responded with increasingly repressive methods to restore order.

## The Growth of the Unions

In 1914, World War I broke out. Although Spain declared itself neutral, the effects of the global conflict on its economy put further strains on a country governed by a discredited and exhausted system. Initially, the war brought about an unexpected boom in the Spanish economy, as it exported products to both sides in the conflict. However, while the owners of businesses pocketed the huge profits, none of the wealth trickled down to the working classes. For many, the war had brought nothing more than rising prices and financial hardship. The government did nothing to improve the situation. Against this background of dissatisfaction, workers swelled the ranks of the UGT and CNT. Between 1917 and 1923, the political and social climate worsened and riots, strikes, and assassinations became the order of the day.

The workers were not the only ones to find it necessary to organize themselves into unions. The army was also affected by economic hardships and inflation. Over the years, it had developed into an enormous immobile bureaucratic entity that had defied any attempts to reform it. Accordingly, life in the army was beset by low salaries and poor conditions. In 1916, mid-ranking officials in the Infantry established their own form of union, the Juntas Militares. This was, in part, an attempt to improve conditions in the army itself, but it was also an attack against the political system—a somewhat worrying development for politicians, little respected by the military who considered itself a victim of their incompetent politics.

In 1917, the government found itself having to contend with a reformist front consisting of regionalists, Socialists, and Republicans. In the growing crisis, Eduardo Dato, the prime minister of the time, responded by simply closing the Cortes. The Catalans were outraged and rebelled. Conservative Catalan leader Francesc Cambó convoked a parliamentary assembly, celebrated in secret in Barcelona, with the objectives of opening the Cortes, ending the *turno pacífico*, and forming a national government. The government treated it as an act of sedition. To secure the backing of the military, Cambó appealed for the support of the Juntas Militares. However, there were two major problems. The army was not disposed to what it considered to be a manifestation of regionalism, nor did it identify with the workers' movements. With his options limited, Cambó was in the extremely vulnerable position of having to rely on the controversial and potentially explosive left for support.

The UGT took the decision to go on strike in support of the reformist front, with little success. Then events came to a head in August, when a general strike was declared; but this time with the participation of the highly revolutionary and anarchistic CNT. The result was a bloody clash between the army and the workers' movements. It came as a profound shock to many politicians who had supported the reformist front, but whose only interest in the unions lay in their use as an instrument of pressure. They had wanted nothing to do with their revolutionary tactics.

The general strike changed the whole matter into a question of law and order. Any meaningful dialogue was over. The army, faithful to the king, had shown its readiness to defend his government; and, at the same time, it had shown itself to be the ultimate force to be reckoned with. It was thanks to the army that the political regime survived, but it was more dependent than ever on the generals to maintain law and order.

# The Disintegration of Law and Order

When the economic boom caused by the war came to end, it brought more conflicts between the workforce and employers, who had now lost an enormous part of their foreign trade. Once again, Catalonia was in the eye of the storm. Government attempts to negotiate with the moderates in the unions were wrecked by the employers. In 1919, the government attempted to settle the strike of the Canadiense, the Canadian electric power company in Barcelona. For more than six weeks the city had been brought to a standstill without electricity or trams. In attempt to resolve the situation, the government accepted demands for an eight-hour working day; but the employees were subsequently prevented from going back to work when their employers imposed a lockout. Violent clashes broke out, with the police and army taking the side of the employers against the unions. The event sparked further hostilities throughout the country. Spain was caught in a spiral of violence as killings took place regularly, and gangs of extremists, known as *pistoleros*, fought each other in bloody street battles. In March 1921, the violence struck at the heart of government with the assassination of the conservative prime minister, Eduardo Dato.

The government was truly beleaguered, but there was more to come. To cap it all, there was a major problem in Morocco. Spain had been engaged in a highly unpopular war against the Rif mountain tribes as it struggled to control its Moroccan protectorate. In the summer of 1921, the Spanish army, which was in retreat, was attacked by a smaller force led by the Rif chieftain Muhammad Abd-el-Krim. It was a disaster. In the carnage that followed, thousands of Spanish army recruits were killed. Spain suffered a devasting and humiliating defeat that scandalized the nation.

In the subsequent search for responsibilty, political opinon in the country was irredeemably divided. The Socialists and opposition attacked the conservatives, under whose administration the disaster had taken place, as well as the king for encouraging the military to act in such an irresponsible and wreckless way; the military blamed the

Muhammad Abd-el-Krim, the Rif chieftain who defeated the Spanish army in Morocco.

politicians for their negligent treatment of the army; and the king, on his part, attacked his ministers for their cowardice and failure to defend him from the attacks of the left

The final desperate act of the regime was the creation of a new liberal government that set out to implement a program of radical constitutional reform. A commission was established in July 1923 to investigate the Moroccan catastrophe, in front of which the king and the army would have to appear. It was too late. In September, the Captain-General of Catalonia, General Miguel Primo de Rivera staged a coup in Barcelona. His *pronunciamiento* was met with absolutely no resistance at all and had the full support of the king. The fact that no one was prepared to defend the government and the parliamentary system was final damning proof of the regime's unpopularity. The army presented itself as unstained by the corrupt system and the only legitimate force capable of maintaining social order and the unity of Spain. In the end, in the face of the inability of the politicians to find a solution, the reply had come from outside the parliamentary system, from a force that ultimately no one could question.

# DICTATORSHIP AND DEMOCRACY IN THE 20TH CENTURY

## The Dictatorship of Primo de Rivera

Miguel Primo de Rivera, Dictator of Spain from 1923 to 1930.

With the Cortes dissolved, the constitution suspended, and political parties banned, Spain was now under a military dictatorship. There had been talk for many years of the need for an "iron surgeon" who would take control of the country, suspend the parliamentary system, and perform the painful operation of forcing through the desperately needed political and economic reforms to modernize the country. Could General Primo de Rivera, who certainly commanded a great deal of popular appeal, be such a "surgeon"?

Under the stability guaranteed by the army, the economy began to pick up again. Primo de Rivera's regime set about attracting foreign capital to set up large companies in key industries and initiated a major program of public works, such as improving roads and modernizing the railway system. On the military front, Primo de Rivera managed to reverse some of the damage inflicted during the "disaster" of 1921, by bringing the Spanish Moroccan protectorate under control and later capturing the infamous Muhammad Abd-el-Krim, the chieftain who had led the devastating attack on the Spain's ill-prepared conscript army.

However, voices of dissent were soon being raised, not just from the various groups that were becoming impatient to take an active role in politics once more, but from many other areas of society as well. Despite promises of returning the country to democracy, Primo de Rivera held back. The dictator was showing himself to be something of a political dabbler, with little inclination to restore the constitution and re-introduce the civil liberties that he had suspended. Furthermore, he had made himself unpopular with the Catalans by his clumsy attempts to stifle the expression of Catalan nationalism. More worrying was his clash with fellow army officers over attempts to reform the Artillery Corps—a situation that led to serious breaches of discipline.

Towards the end of the decade, the economy was showing signs of trouble and a growing dissatisfaction amongst the workers was expressed in the increasing number of strikes that were being called. The Socialist union, the UGT, which had co-operated with the dictatorship, withdrew its support for the regime in 1929. The Wall Street Crash that same year, which plunged the world markets into crisis, pushed Spain further into economic hardship and growing unemployment. No longer confident of the full support of the army, the struggling dictator read the warning signs—it was time for him to go. In January 1930, Primo de Rivera offered his resignation to the king, who readily accepted it, and left for Paris. He died in self-imposed exile a few months later, a deeply disappointed man.

## The Exile of the King

With Primo de Rivera gone, a power vacuum opened up that subjected Spain to the same anguish that had been so familiar in the previous century. At first, King Alfonso XIII hoped that the dictatorship would be forgotten and things would get back to how they had been before. To this end, the king entrusted a general, Dámaso Berenguer, to set about restoring the constitution and re-opening the Cortes. Yet Alfonso XIII, whose own support was at an all-time low, had not counted on the strength and organization of the growing anti-monarchist movement throughout the country. Predominantly consisting of groups on the left, but also including many others such as Catalan nationalists, the anti-monarchists came together and made a pact to bring about the end of the monarchy and establish a republic. A period of instability followed as the pro- and anti-monarchists sized each other up; and in Aragón there was a failed *pronunciamiento* in support of a republic. Knowing that he could not command sufficient public support, Berenguer had no option but to resign. A new government was established. From the results of municipal elections held at the time, it was clear that,

Alfonso XIII followed by Primo de Rivera— both men lost the support of the Army and the nation.

despite support for the king in rural areas, the Republican-Socialist coalition was clearly the favorite in the big cities. Amidst fears of a popular uprising, Alfonso had become a liability. Few were prepared to risk a bloodbath in favor of a king whose reign had been characterized by a continuous display of poor judgment and weakness of character. Without the clear support of the army, there was little more to be done. On the evening of April 14, 1931, abandoned by the nation, Alfonso XIII fled the country. Shortly afterwards the Second Spanish Republic was declared.

## The Second Spanish Republic and the Republican-Socialist Reforms

The Second Spanish Republic was welcomed by many who saw the chance of a new beginning in Spain—anything was possible it seemed.

Elections to establish a republican parliament in the summer of 1931 resulted in the overwhelming victory of the Republican-Socialist coalition. A new constitution was drafted and approved, and both men and women were given the right to vote. The existing two-chamber system of parliament was abandoned in favor of one that housed the elected deputies. Individual liberties were guaranteed including freedom of expression, association, and religious worship. Between 1931 and 1933, under the administration of Prime Minister Manuel Azaña, an eloquent chain-smoking politician with a penchant for translating classic writers such as Charles Dickens and Voltaire, the government attempted to implement a whole range of reforms. From the very beginning, those responsible for creating the Second Republic in Spain—principally the Socialists and Republicans of the left—worked with a great deal of caution. They were well aware that the reforms necessary to drag the country from the clutches of the past had to be brought about by means of parliamentary process—in other words, they needed the approval of the Cortes.

Manuel Azaña, Prime Minister (1931-1933)
of the Second Spanish Republic.

Yet reforming the country meant challenging the status quo. Neither the Church, the army, nor the traditional landowners could be permitted to escape the sweeping new changes. It was widely acknowledged that army needed to be modernized. A major problem that desperately needed to be addressed was the huge number of military officers in its ranks. In an attempt to reduce it, Azaña introduced a number of measures, which included offering officers early voluntary paid retirement. But, unlike with his other reforms, Azaña introduced the new army laws by decree instead of waiting for the approval of the Cortes. Thus there was little parliamentary discussion; and the army was deprived of its say in the fundamental changes that were affecting it. It was a decision that would come back to haunt the Republic. The message, it seemed, was clear—Azaña had no faith in his generals. His actions had left the military critics of the Republic with a perfect excuse to portray it as an enemy of the army.

There was a great deal of pressure on the government from the left to reform the antiquated system of land ownership. In many regions, conditions in the countryside had not changed for hundreds of years. Landless peasants were at the mercy of the wealthy landowners who ran huge inefficient states. Peasants faced six months of meager wages for working their lands followed by six months of semi-starvation during the off-season period. But attempts to dismantle the system and ease the dire conditions were doomed to fail. Under the new laws approved by the Cortes in 1932, the state had the right to confiscate lands over a certain size, or those which were not being cultivated, but it would have to offer compensation. However, there was a dilemma. The success of the scheme depended on the funds available to compensate the landowners, but the government had no cash. Furthermore, there was little agreement as to how to divide the land—the Socialists preferred collective holdings and the Republicans individual plots. The end result was that very little land was actually redistributed and very few landless peasants actually received the promised new land. The whole situation was compounded by the great world Depression, which came as an unfortunate handicap to the new Republic. According to some estimates, the number of unemployed rose from 389,000 in 1932 to 801,322 in June 1936—of whom more than half were farm workers. The situation was made worse by the return of many Spanish immigrants who had recently lost their jobs in other countries.

The government's attempted reforms to improve labor conditions were sabotaged by the big landowners of the south. They either ignored the laws, resorting to violent means to impose their will, or they used their influence in the Cortes in order to obstruct the reforms. The anarcho-syndical organizations such as the CNT responded with a campaign of revolutionary strikes. These actions had two consequences. Firstly, they fed the propaganda of the landowners, who were painting the politicians of the Republic as little more than puppets of Soviet Communism—a successful move that helped them gain the support of the smaller frightened landowners around the country. Secondly, the government's tough response to the anarchists created tensions in the fragile relationship between the Socialists and Republicans. When the CNT declared a national strike in January 1933, the government launched a violent attack on peasant rebels in the poverty-stricken southern village of Casas Viejas, massacring twenty-five. This act, together with the patent lack of progress made in agrarian reforms, was enough to discredit the Republicans in the eyes of the Socialists and brought an end to the collaboration between the two sides.

The treatment of the Church was one of the most controvesial actions of the government. The Church, seen by the left as part of the old order and a potential danger to the Republic, was stripped of its special status as the state religion. In other words, Spain was no longer an officially Catholic country but a secular state. State grants to the Church were cut, divorce was legalized, and the Jesuits again disbanded. In the new Republic, education was to be secularized and religious images banned from the classrooms. The reforms were divisive. The Church raged against what it declared was state persecution. It was not just the staunch conservatives who were shocked. There was a feeling amongst the Catholic middle class, which was by and large highly supportive of the Republic, that the government was passing over their interests in favor of the Socialists and the anticlerical non-Catholic working class.

The constitutional attacks played a key role in the unification of Catholic sentiment, be it moderate or extreme, thus creating a common cause to defend a persecuted Church. The clause that prohibited religious orders from teaching in schools was an attack on the ideology of the traditional ruling class. It was this dissatisfaction, aggravated by spontaneous anticlerical protests, that led, in February 1933, to the creation of the popular party, the Confederación Española de Derechas Autonomas (CEDA). A coalition of various parties on the right, its objective was a revision of the constitution and the defense of Catholic principals. It was this party, led by José María Gil Robles, that played a key role in defeating Azaña's government and reversing practically all that it had done. With the economy in a bad state and social conditions worsening, things were going desperately wrong. Faced with growing opposition, Azaña resigned as head of government in September 1933. The president of the Republic, Niceto Alcalá Zamora, subsequently called elections.

## The Two Black Years

In the elections of November 1933, which saw the Socialists withdraw their support for the Republicans and mass abstentions by the CNT, the right-wing coalition CEDA gained a majority in the Cortes. From the very outset, there was a great deal of suspicion over its leader's position towards the Republic. Gil Robles, a known admirer of Adolf Hitler, strongly believed in giving the Church a pivotal role in the state. For him, the form of government was of secondary importance. Despite his apparent commitment to working within the law, his leadership was compromised by its financial and electoral dependence on conservative groups that had little confidence or respect for legal methods. Owing to such distrust, President Alcalá Zamora blocked the formation of a CEDA government. Instead, the middle-class backed center party, Partido Radical, headed by Alejandro Lerroux, formed a government.

Nevertheless, CEDA ministers were to exert a great deal of influence over Lerroux's government; and its demands to participate in goverment were to unleash a great deal of hostility. During a period referred to as "The Two Black Years" (*Bienio Negro*), the right began to reverse many of the reforms.

The thorny issue of regionalism was yet another area that threatened to destabilize the country. The new constitution recognized the principal of regional autonomy, and the Catalans were quick to take advantage. They promptly established their own elected regional parliament and gave Catalán the status of an official language. In all matters—except those relating to law enforcement, the army, and foreign affairs—the region was theoretically free to do as it wished.

Owing to the fact that it had a Socialist majority in its parliament, Catalonia initially managed to keep the right-wing at bay. However, conflicts emerged between the left and the right over a new law to allow winegrowers in the region to buy the lands that, until now, they had leased. The landowners were incensed at this attack on their property and, after appealing to the consitutional court, had the law declared unconstitutional. In an act of defiance, the Catalan government ignored the ruling and upheld the law.

This amounted to more than just a conflict between left and right— it was a symptom of the centrifugal forces exerted by the regions on the center. The Catalan government had directly challenged the authority of the goverment in the capital. The question of regionalism complicated and confused the traditional divisions between class and ideology. This was especially the case in the Basque Country, a region that was a bastion of Catholicism. Many Basques found themselves torn between CEDA, which promised to uphold religious values but supported strong central government, and the Republican left, which promised the region the autonomy it so much desired.

Hostility towards CEDA resulted in a major crisis during October 1934, with the entry of three CEDA ministers into the cabinet of the government. The event caused uproar. The Republicans railed at the prospect of permitting members of the party to participate in government when their program was clearly unconstitutional and was headed down the road of corporate state. This was a point of no return for the nation: it was at this point that the dividing lines for the Civil War were drawn.

The crisis sparked off a revolt in Asturias and Catalonia, known as the "October Revolution." In Barcelona, the leader of the Catalan government, Lluis Companys, declared the independence of the State of Catalonia within a Federal Republic of Spain—an act of defiance that was quickly quashed by the government. In Asturias, members of the Alianza Obrera, an alliance between the UGT and CNT, staged an uprising. In order to suppress the rebellion, the government called on the help of the army. Under the command of General Francisco Franco, troops of the Spanish Legion, aided by Moroccan mercenaries, ruthlessly put down the uprising. Around 2,000 people were killed. After quelling the rebellion, the government lashed out with a wave of reprisals that left many more dead. Jails swelled with activists and many left-wing politicians—in all there were around 30,000 prisoners, including the ex-prime minister of the Republic, Azaña, and the UGT leader Francisco Largo Caballero. Although a failure, the uprising was mythologized by the workers. At the same time—helped by an effective propaganda campaign—it came as a profound shock to the middle and upper classes.

In the aftermath of the October Revolution, the government, by now under the thumb of CEDA, began to annul or reverse the reforms wholesale. The Catalan Statute of Autonomy was suspended on December 14, 1934. In August 1935, new agrarian reforms were introduced that overturned those of 1932. Even the attempts to usher in minor social reforms by a moderate CEDA minister, Giménez Fernández, came to nothing—he was dismissed by his own side as a Communist stooge.

## Militancy and the Rejection of Parliamentary Means

The reforms in ruins, the Socialists in prison, regionalist dreams smothered, and a government whose strings were being pulled by fascists and bolstered by the army—all these were factors in the creation of an alliance, the Frente Popular (Popular Front) that aimed to unite forces on the left in order to save the Republic. It was the victory of this alliance in the elections of February 1936, contested in an atmosphere of great hostility, that marked the end of the right's faith in the CEDA leader Gil Robles, as well as any hopes of imposing its will through parliamentary means. Abandoning Robles as their spokesmen in the Cortes, they began to turn openly to the militant extremists to put an end once and for all to the Republic.

The right pinned its hopes on the Bloque Nacional (National Bloc), founded in 1934 by the monarchist José Calvo Sotelo, whose intention was to militarily restore Alfonso XIII to the throne. Others favored the more extreme fascist-inspired Falange Party or, alternatively, the Carlist Party, which had its own militia based in Navarra.

Developments on the left further aggravated an already explosive situation. The two most influential Socialist leaders, Indalecio Prieto and Largo Caballero, could not see eye to eye. Prieto argued for Socialist collaboration in the new Republican government. Largo Caballero, preoccupied by the possibility of losing the support of the workers, spoke out against this position and began to take a more and more revolutionary stance. His position denied the Republicans much of the support they needed to form a strong government. The moderate center ground was being disastrously eroded as supporters scrambled to the far left and far right.

A period of escalating violence began, with confrontations between militant elements on both sides. Furthermore, a wave of strikes, principally by the CNT, added fuel to the fire and contributed to the rapid degeneration of public order, creating a pervasive climate of fear.

## The Military Solution

The last hundred years of Spanish history had clearly demonstrated the all too frequent tendency of the military to intervene in politics and exercise its role as final arbiter. Cánovas had created the 1876 constitution specifically to avoid the problem; but his scheme had ultimately failed when General Primo de Rivera staged his coup in 1923. And both Primo de Rivera and King Alfonso XIII were doomed to a life of exile once they had lost the clear backing of the army.

Although the military was not openly hostile to the Republic, there were certainly rumblings of discontent. Azaña's military reforms had done nothing to endear the Republic to the army, and he was accused by some of wanting to crush it. Furthermore, certain military officers had been involved in monarchist conspiracies, including a failed

José Calvo Sotello, assassinated by the Republicans.

coup attempt in 1932. But it was not until the the victory of the Frente Popular and the deterioration of public order that the army was finally provoked into taking full-scale action.

The center of the military conspiracy was the Unión Militar Española. Through this organization, links were established with monarchist groups and the Falange; and after much deliberation, the plotters took the momentous decision in March to bring down the Republican government.

In spite of many warnings about the dangers of an imminent coup, the government did little to protect itself. In fact it made matters worse by transferring the leader of the plot, General Mola, to the home territory of the monarchist Carlist party in Navarra, where he was anything but out of the way.

On July 13, amidst the frequent episodes of violence, the leader of the Bloque National, José Calvo Sotelo, was assassinated in retaliation for the murder of a Republican police officer. It was an act that removed the doubts of any waverers.

Just two days earlier, an ex-British Royal Air Force pilot, Captain Cecil Bebb, unaware of his true mission, had flown his airplane from Croydon airport, outside of London, to the Canary Islands. Once there, he had picked up a charter passenger, and had continued onward to the military base of military base of Melilla in Spanish Morroco.

His passenger was General Francisco Franco, whose objective was to assume command of the Spanish African Army and to stage a military insurrection against the Republic. Captain Bebb, who had merely accepted the job as a dare and took two female friends with him, was hired because attempts to find a suitable civil aircraft in Spain had drawn a blank. On July 17, slightly ahead of Franco's arrival, the army mutinied in Melilla—an act that marked the beginning of one of the cruelest and bloodiest of civil wars.

It was clear that the Republic had failed—incapable of controlling the extraparliamentary forces of the left or right—the latter of which, having no success in overthrowing the regime by legal methods, opted for a military solution. The conservative forces of the right had played their trump card, calling on the many disgruntled officers in the army who had been waiting in the wings, ready to step in to save Spain from what they perceived as corrupt and inept politicians who had allowed the country to fall into chaos.

# The Spanish Civil War

Immediately after the *pronunciamiento* was issued, the army swiftly secured many areas that had voted for the right in the elections, especially in northern and central areas of Spain, including Galicia, León, Salamanca, Castilla, and the traditional Carlist strongholds of Navarra and Aragón. In the south, the offensive was undertaken by the Spanish Legion, which under the command of General Franco, had crossed the Strait of Gibraltar. In October 1936, Franco was named head of state and *generalísimo*, the supreme commander of the combined military forces. He was to prove to be a formidable enemy.

Francisco Franco Bahamonde was born in Galicia in 1892, into an extremely religious military family. He had made his career in the Moroccan wars, becoming a general in 1926, at the almost unheard of age of 33. He was a tough man with nerves of steel whose strengths lay

General Francisco Franco, leader of the Nationalist forces
during the Civil War.

in his military skills—a fact that earned a great deal of respect from the
army. As head of the what was now referred to as the Nationalist
government, Franco attempted to bring all the right-wing groups into a
single political entity—no voices of dissent would be tolerated. For this
purpose, he united the extremist Falange and Carlist Parties with the
rest of the Nationalist groups under an umbrella party called the
Falange Española Tradicionalista y de las JONS, which later became
know as the Movimiento Nacional.

The original Falange, which had been modeled on Mussolini's own
fascist party in Italy, had been created by General Primo de Rivera's son,
José Antonio. In the early stages of the war, José Antonio, a highly

charismatic leader, was shot by the Republicans. He immediately became a martyr for the Nationalist cause—a situation that Franco exploited to the fullest.

Taking Sevilla and Córdoba in the south, Franco's forces pushed northwards through a wide corridor along the western side of Spain, until they joined with the Nationalists in the north. Despite hopes of taking Madrid, the city held out. From November 1936 until the last days of the Civil War in March 1939, the city defended itself against air bombardments, artillery attacks, and every other means of destruction the Nationalists had to throw at it.

By October 1937, after the Nationalists had taken control of the northern territories west of the Pyrenees, Spain was dramatically split in two. With the Nationalists to the west, the Republicans held the east of Spain from Barcelona in the north to Almeria in the south, as well as a good deal of the center of the country including Madrid.

The Republicans were at a major military disadvantage. Apart from a few members of the armed forces who remained loyal to the Republic, the vast majority of its army was made up of inexperienced recruits who lacked decent training and equipment. Unlike the Nationalists, the Republic found little in the way of international support. The only country that supplied the Republicans with significant aid was Russia. Extra help from International Brigades made up of volunteers, many of whom held strong Socialist convictions and felt an affinity with the Republic in its fight against the forces of fascism, did more to boost morale rather than increase the chances of military victory. France made a token gesture and supplied some aircraft and artillery. Britain and the USA on the other hand, imposed an arms embargo on Spain. Starved of vital military equipment, the Republic's huge army could only postpone the inevitable.

The Nationalists were much more fortunate. Counting on not only almost the whole of the regular Spanish army, they also received vital support from the fascist regimes of Germany and Italy. Franco made use of both of these country's airforces to airlift his troops from Africa into Spain. It was also in Spain that the bombers of Adolf Hitler's Condor

Civil War—the Nationalist and Republican division towards the end of 1937.

Legion perfected the deadly techniques used later by the German Luftwaffe in the Second World War. In one terrible air bombardment, in April 1937, they utterly destroyed Guernica—an ancient town that had come to symbolize the Basque spirit of independence. The event inspired and gave its name to one the greatest works by the Spanish painter, Pablo Picasso. Added to this, both Hitler and Mussolini sent large fully equipped and trained divisions into Spain to fight alongside the Nationalists.

The Republicans had to contend with more than the fight against the Nationalists. There were serious divisions in their own ranks that seriously undermined their ability to form a united and effective military force. Although the anarchists were on the Republican side, the truth was they cared little for its instutions and had a quite different picture of the future. Their goal was ultimately the overthrow of the state, *any* state. In the midst of civil war they pursued their revolutionary agenda, taking over over factories, businesses and land, and proceeding to collectivize them. The Republican government, headed by the Socialist Largo Caballero, did what it could to control the anarchists and other extremists. In the end it was the Communists, whose own revolutionary aims were put on hold to pursue the war against the Nationalists, who used their considerable influence to get the government to create a regular army and who put an end to the chaotic array of independent extremist militias. Those who continued to defy the central government found themselves on the receiving end of ruthless campaigns of suppression organized by the Communists who would tolerate no rivalry.

Largo Caballero's successor, the Communist-backed Socialist Juan Negrín, failed to impose the high level of organization on the Republican forces that might have given them a chance against the disciplined Nationalist army. As it was, Franco's forces were unstoppable. In 1938, the Nationalists pushed east from Teruel all the way to the Mediterranean, securing the coastal region from above Valencia to the mouth of the River Ebro, and cutting Catalonia off from the Republic. Catalonia finally fell to the Nationalists at the beginning of 1939, and with it all Republican hopes vanished. The Republican government was forced to flee to France.

A call to arms by the huge anarchist organization CNT during
the early days of the Civil War.

In Madrid, meanwhile, things seemed hopeless as factional fighting broke out amongst those who were supposed to be defending the city from the Nationalists. All the Republicans could do was hold out in the hope that war in Europe would break out against Germany. This, it was hoped, would bring the French and British into the conflict. But it was too late. At the end of March, the Republican military command, faced with complete chaos in the city, took control of the city and surrendered it to the Nationalists. On April 1, Franco declared the end of the Civil War. It marked the end of the Republican experiment and the beginning of what was to be a long and troubled dictatorship.

During the horror of the Civil War it has been estimated that some 600,000 people lost their lives. One particularly gruesome aspect of the conflict was the number of executions carried out by both sides. Thousands upon thousands of victims, accused of aiding the enemy, were mercilessly taken out and shot by Republican and Nationalist firing squads alike. Many, many more were to die at the hands of Franco's executioners in the aftermath of the war. One tragic victim of the frenzy of killing was the writer Federico García Lorca.

## García Lorca and the Soul of the Gypsy

Federico García Lorca was an enormously popular poet and playwright during his lifetime, and today holds a special place in 20th-century Spanish literature. He was born to a well-off Andalusian family in 1898, in the village of Fuente Vaqueros, Granada. Although apparently destined for a career in law, he abandoned this in order to study what he loved most—literature, art, and music. Attending the University of Madrid, he stayed in the *Residencia de Estudiantes* (Residence of Scholars) where he met other writers and painters and struck up an enduring friendship with a young artist who would become recognized the world over, Salvador Dalí.

The key source of García Lorca's inspiration was his native Andalucía. Its culture and gypsy folklore provided him with the raw material from which to conjure up magical scenes that continue to weave their spell on readers today— works such as "Poema del Cante Jondo" ("Poem of Deep Song") written in 1922, and "Romancero Gitano" ("The Gypsy Ballad").

Federico García Lorca.

García Lorca was especially fascinated by *cante jondo* (deep song), a traditional Andalusian musical form that forms an integral part of flamenco. Although the name flamenco first begins to appear in writing in the 1770s, its roots stretch much further back in time. Its distinct sound evolved in a region with a rich cultural history, a fascinating product of the local Islamic heritage, gypsy culture, and popular songs and dances.

García Lorca also took a great interest in the theater. At the outset of the Republic, he was appointed a director of the state-funded traveling theater, *La Barraca* (*The Barrack*), which gave poor peasants and working classes around the country the opportunity to see classic plays. His own plays have become classics in their own right. Works such as *Bodas de Sangre* (*Blood Wedding*)—a folk tragedy that tells the story of a bride's abduction by her former sweetheart on her wedding day—is a fine example of García Lorca's gift for the genre, showing a whole array of influences and leaning towards surrealism, yet still deeply rooted in Andalusian folklore.

García Lorca's reputation spread beyond his own country, and he subsequently spent some time traveling abroad. However, he was never happy at being far away from the place he loved most— Andalucía. Indeed, during a stay in the United States, his sense of alienation became acute and led him to compose a cycle of poems entitled *Poeta en Nueva York* (*A Poet in New York*). Written between 1929 and 1930, García Lorca uses powerful images to convey his sense of despair of the brutal and mechanized modern society. The modern American city was a far cry from his native land.

Lorca's close bond with Andalucía proved to be his tragic undoing. In 1936, at the onset of the Civil War, Lorca announced he would return to Granada, believing he would be safe. Shortly after his arrival there, he was seized by the Nationalists on account of his liberal ideas and connections with left-wing intellectuals. In the middle of the night he was taken out and shot—a senseless act, yet one that was typical of the arbitrary justice meted out during the terrible conflict.

# Two Giants of the World of Art—Picasso and Dalí

The Civil War touched everyone's life in Spain, and two of the country's most influential figures in the world of modern art, Pablo Picasso and Lorca's good friend, Salvador Dalí, also found the course of their lives altered by the events of the 1930s.

The life of Pablo Picasso, arguably the most important artist in 20th century art and certainly amongst the most controversial, began in Málaga in 1881. The son of an art teacher, Picasso excelled in art as a child. At the age of 15, he passed the entrance examinations to the School of Fine Arts in Barcelona with flying colors.

Things began to fall into place for the young artist during his early twenties when he made a series of visits to Paris. There he soaked up the lively atmosphere of the city and met a variety of artists and avant-garde writers. It was during this time, between 1901 and 1904 that he produced the paintings of his "Blue" period, so-called because of the dominance of the color in his work. Melancholic in mood, they reflected his sensitivity to the world of society's underdogs, such as prostitutes, beggars, and drunks. After deciding to settle in Paris, Picasso developed his "Rose" period, a warmer and more optimistic body of work dominated by reds and pinks. Amongst his favorite subjects at the time were circus performers and dancers.

Yet it was "Cubism," a movement created by Picasso and the French artist Georges Braque, that was to revolutionize painting and sculpture in the 20th century. Cubism—so named after an art critic disparagingly remarked that a painting by Braque was little more than a collection of "bizarre cubes"—rejected the naturalistic tradition in art. Instead of attempting to create the illusion of reality by using conventional methods, it broke objects down to geometrical units. Furthermore, where once objects were presented from a single perspective, now they were shown from a variety of viewpoints at the same time.

During the Civil War, Picasso's sympathies lay squarely with the Republicans. At the outset of the conflict he was appointed director of the Prado Museum (which housed the greatest collection of art in Spain) by the Republican government. It was a symbolic act that was clearly designed to rile the conservative Nationalists.

The Republican government also approached Picasso to create a mural for the Spanish Pavilion in the 1937 Paris World Fair. His inspiration was not far in coming. The terrible destruction of the Basque town of Guernica in 1937 on the orders of Franco galvanized Picasso into creating one of his most famous works of art. Although an unusual and highly complex painting, *Guernica* clearly conveys the artist's sense of outrage and revulsion towards the tragic event, featuring figures whose mouths are open in what has been described as an "unheard scream."

That same year, Picasso went to Paris to exhibit *Guernica*—he would never again return to his native Spain. Like so many of his fellow Spaniards, he was fated to live in exile. Still in France during the Second World War, Picasso became a member of the Communist Party. For him, it represented the fight against the evils of fascism—a party that had opposed Franco and played an important role in the French resistance movement during the occupation by the Germans. It was a move that would ensure Picasso's lasting reputation as the *bête noire* of the Franco regime.

An opponent of Franco to the end, Picasso stipulated that *Guernica* should only be returned to Spain after the death of Franco and the restoration of civil liberties in the country. For many years the work was exhibited in the Museum of Modern Art in New York. It was only in 1981 that Picasso's conditions were met and the picture returned to Spain. It is now housed in the Centro de Arte Reina Sofia in Madrid. After a long and fruitful life, Picasso died in France in 1973, at the age of 91.

Another giant in the world of modern art was Picasso's fellow-countryman, Salvador Dalí. Dalí was born in 1904, in the Catalan town of Figueres. During his lifetime, he became internationally famous, almost as much for his outrageous and extravagant behavior—often craftily employed as a means to generate self-publicity—as for his splendid art. He himself once said: "The only difference between myself and a madman is that I am not mad."

In the early part of his career he became familiar with the work of Picasso and another great Spanish artist, the Surrealist Joan Miró—both of whom he had met. The two artists exerted a great influence on the young Dalí—especially Miró, a highly imaginative artist that employed a spontaneous style intended to bring the unconscious workings of the mind to the surface. However, by the 1930s, Dalí had developed his own unique style, producing startling works which were remarkable for their hallucinatory dream images and suffused with psychological symbolism.

During the Civil War, Dalí moved to Paris and then, in 1940, to the USA, where he continued to work and exhibit his paintings. Unlike Picasso who had taken a clear stand in the Civil War, Dalí was a waverer. Although apparently tending towards the side of the Republicans at the beginning, he seemingly moved over to the Nationalist camp as Franco gained the upper hand. Whereas Picasso could quite clearly live the life of an ex-patriot, Dalí could not envision a future spent in exile. He always yearned for his native Catalonia, and in 1948 made the decision to return.

A few years later, Dalí shocked the opponents of the Nationalist regime and many of his contemporaries in the art world, when, during a lecture in Madrid, he expressed his outright support for Franco, whom he declared had rescued the country from the disorder and ruin brought about the politicians and imposed "clarity, truth, and order" on Spain.

He was also critical of Picasso's absence from Spain along with his political beliefs, and at the same lecture stated: "As always, Spain has the honor of producing the greatest contrasts, this case in the form of the two most antagonistic artists of modern painting—Picasso and myself, your humble servant. Picasso is Spanish, so am I. Picasso is a genius, so am I. Picasso is about 72, I'm about 48. Picasso is known in every country in the world, so am I. Picasso is a Communist, I am not."

Dalí died in 1989, a contoversial figure until the end, yet he is held with great respect as an artist by the Spanish people and his work continues to be a great cause for celebration. Although many of his works hang in a variety of art museums, some of his most unusual creations can be seen in the Teatre-Museu Dalí, in his birthplace of Figueres, which the artist himself converted into what has now almost become his own shrine.

# Franco's Dictatorship—The Early Years

In 1939, after three tragic years of Civil War, Spain emerged as a new nation under a dictatorship. For the next 36 years, until his death in 1975, the country would know no other leader than General Franco, the supreme head of state. Victory belonged to the traditional forces of the country, and Franco saw to it that all traces of the Republic were eliminated. The two pillars of the state were now the Military and the Church. Apart from the Movimiento Nacional, all parties in Spain were outlawed. No person, group, or region that had sided with the Republic could expect forgiveness. Many were shot, sentenced to hard labor, or forced into exile. Teachers, writers, artists, and others who were representative of the liberal spirit of the Republic fled the country in waves—perhaps as many as half a million. They were simply not welcome, nor would their ideas be tolerated.

The Nationalists had drawn on the myths of the reconquest of Spain from the Muslims and likened the Civil War to a Crusade against the godless republic. The Church was now to be given back the central role that the Republic had taken away. Education was entrusted once again to the clergy; divorce was prohibited; and no marriage could take place outside the Catholic Church.

Having gained power, it remained to be seen if Franco could hold onto it and weather the first few tricky years. Yet, the dictator avoided the mistake of basing his regime on an inflexible ideology, and showed

General Franco.

himself to be pragmatic enough to allow changes that defused potential conflict but did not in any way upset the foundations of the state.

A threat to Franco's rule came from close supporters of the general during the Civil War. These were the groups who had hoped for a return of the monarchy. With the death of Alfonso XIII in 1941, the next in line to throne was his son Juan de Bourbon. Conspirators secretly hatched plans to place Juan on the throne, hoping in vain that they might find international support from the Allied forces fighting the war in Europe.

Several years later, in 1947, Franco pre-empted the monarchists by declaring Spain to be a kingdom once again, which he did after canvassing the opinion of the nation in a plebiscite. Yet Franco reserved the right to choose his own king to succeed him when he pleased.

Franco's plan was to have not Juan, but his son Juan Carlos as heir. The dictator managed to persuade Juan to send his young son to Spain to be educated under his watchful eye. By addressing the issue of the monarchy and succession, he had to some degree managed to legitimize own rule. But Franco, excercising his prerogative as the ultimate authority, was in no hurry to declare a successor—and when he did

officially proclaim Juan Carlos as his heir in 1969, it was only because he was sure he had chosen a man who would continue his regime after his death.

In its early days, the new dictatorship was in an internationally precarious postition owing to the fact that it had relied on the support of the fascist dicatorships of Germany and Italy for its victory. With the Second World War raging in Europe, Spain was thus still closely indentified with the fascists. However, Franco steered clear of involving Spain directly in the war, despite the wishes of pro-German elements in his government. After the

Juan de Bourbon, who was never to be a king. Franco chose his son Juan Carlos to be the future monarch of Spain.

involvement of the USA in the war, which made the possibility of Germany's defeat more likely, Franco stuck to the path of neutrality. He was careful not to do anything likely to precipitate trouble with the Anglo-US alliance.

## Isolation and the Failed Economics of Self-Sufficiency

Life for many during the first years of the Franco dictatorship was one of extreme hardship—it was a period known as "The Years of Hunger." The Civil War had left Spain's economy in ruins—its industry and infrastructure were severely disrupted. The damaging effects of the Second World War on the global economy made matters worse. Furthermore, Franco's close reliance on the fascist powers led to Spain's isolation after the war. Whereas other Western European countries had access to the US-funded Marshall Plan, which supplied the vital aid needed to restore their war-torn economies, Spain was excluded. The acute shortages of even the most basic foodstuffs, along with petrol and other important products, required strict rationing in Spain—a situation that continued until the beginning of the 1950s. A flourishing blackmarket grew as a select minority made huge profits by selling scarce products at many times the official prices.

In an attempt to tackle the economic hardships, Franco instigated the policy of autarky—a system based on the principle of national self-sufficiency. Laws were introduced that favored firms considered to be of major national interest. These were granted privileges to encourage them to produce goods that would otherwise have been imported. Furthermore, firms that received state support were themselves required to use domestically produced products whenever possible. Finally, a whole range of measures were introduced to make imports less attractive, such as high tariffs for goods entering the country and exchange rate controls. Through the National Institute of Industry, the state also took a direct role in developing key national industries. Yet the policies were unsuccessful in bringing about the desired effects, and failed to bring the economy up to its pre-Civil War levels. By the late 1950s, the country was facing bankruptcy.

## Spain's Emergence from Isolation

Spain gradually began to emerge from a decade of isolation in the 1950s. With the onset of the Cold War, in which the Western powers waged a battle of ideologies with the Communist world, Spain was no longer viewed in the same way. In the war against Communism, Franco had impeccable credentials—after all he was vehemently anti-Communist and had crushed the Communist movement in his own country. Besides, the Nationalist victory was seen by many as a victory of religion over atheism. Then there was the question of Spain's strategic position at the entrance to the Mediterranean, which could not be ignored by the West. Franco was careful to exploit the situation and in

1951, formed a new government to present a better face to the international community.

A number of significant events took place in the 1950s that improved Spain's international standing. In 1950, the United Nations lifted sanctions it had imposed on the country. Then, in 1953, came Franco's much desired opening up of relations with the USA. That year, the two countries signed a military pact, that allowed the USA to establish military airbases on Spanish territory in return for financial and economic aid. Two years later, in an act that brought the country firmly into the bosom of the international community, Spain joined the United Nations.

## The Economic Miracle

Economic problems continued to blight Spain, however, and by the end of the 1950s, it was suffering from the effects of several years of spiraling inflation. Now with a huge trade-balance deficit, the country had suspended payments of its foreign debts and was facing bankruptcy. It was time for a new breed of players to step in and take over the running of the economy. These were the technocrats, who were closely linked to the Opus Dei, a highly influential semi-secret Catholic organization founded in Spain in the 1920s. The Opus Dei, which was highly conservative, believed that much needed economic reforms could be achieved without having to alter the existing political system. In other words, their plan for the economy would theoretically leave Franco's dictatorship intact.

From the late 1950s on, members of the Opus Dei took over key ministerial posts; and in 1959, they put in into action an economic stabilization plan. This included a wide range of financial measures aimed at bringing prices under control, attending to the huge trade-balance deficit, and doing all they could to encourage competitiveness in the foreign market. What they were looking for most was integration into the European market. The effects on the country were profound. Throughout the 1960s and into the 1970s, Spain witnessed an astonishing economic and social transformation.

As the technocrats tore down the system of self-sufficiency, huge amounts of foreign capital flooded into Spain, forty percent of which came from US investors. The country's industrial output rocketed. Amongst the most successful areas were were car manufacturing, construction materials, electrical equipment, steel and shipyards. The only other country to match Spain's economic growth at the time was Japan.

In addition to massive foreign investment, another external force contributed to the almost miraculous development. This was tourism. As Western Europeans became more prosperous, they had more money to spend on holidays. With the beginning of mass tourism, Spain, with its extensive beautiful Mediterranean coast and warm sunny climate was, and of course still is, an ideal holiday destination. In the 1950s, only a couple of million tourists a year visited the country—a figure that rose to around six million at the beginning of the 1960s. During the next decade and a half, there was an explosion as the figure jumped to around 35 and then to 43 million—more than the entire population of Spain.

Agriculture, however, did not enjoy the same level of success and continued to show the same tenacious resistance to reforms that it had always done. Franco had restored the power of the landed elite as a reward for their loyalty; and these wealthy proprietors were not readily going to approve of plans that would lead to the expropriation of their lands, no matter how unproductive they were accused of being. For the conservatives, the countryside had always been, and continued to remain, a bastion of traditional and "wholesome" values. Although attitudes were to change and reforms did eventually come, it would be a slow process. Productivity would remain low for years to come. However, agriculture by no means remained immune to the industrial boom. Drawn by the promise of work, waves of rural laborers abandoned the countryside and flooded into the industrial areas. In the process, many small-scale farms disappeared.

For those who did not find work in the country's industries there was another option—emigration. France, Switzerland, and West

# Dictatorship and Democracy

Germany absorbed millions of Spanish economic migrants. Principally employed as unskilled laborers, they became an important source of foreign earnings for Spain as they sent home their hard-earned savings. The drain on the rural population as a result of internal and overseas migration sometimes led to the phenomenon of ghost villages, abandoned by all except the old.

The technocrats had promised to transform the economy without rocking the political system. In the process, however, they had unleashed forces far beyond their control. It was becomingly increasingly difficult to reconcile a country that had opened up to the world and boasted an ever more confident and wealthier urban middle class with a political system that was rooted firmly in the past. Franco's regime was running into difficulties. The upshot of it all was that major socio-economic changes were taking place, but the political system, which stood like a huge institutional monument to the Nationalist victory in the Civil War, was out of step. Furthermore, old ghosts had come back to haunt the conservatives—those of Communism and regionalism.

In the early days, Franco had ruthlessly stamped out the labor unions and many of their leaders were either shot, imprisoned, or forced to flee the country. Labor disputes were settled under the watchful eye of the government and the only legal labor organization, the Organización Sindical. But the new economic boom had brought new tensions, as it failed to bring even development across the country. Many were failing to benefit from the new wealth and, with their dissatisfaction, came a revival of working-class industrial action. Illegal unions, known as Comisiones Obreras (Workers' Commissions) mushroomed throughout the country. With the backing of the similarly outlawed Communists, the Comisiones Obreras set about working within the legal the framework of the Organización Sindical to exert pressure on the management and win concessions for their members. This saw a resurgence of strikes which, although illegal, became commonplace from the 1960s onwards.

# Basque Nationalism and ETA

The most serious threat to the regime came from an upsurge of regional nationalism, especially on the part of the Basque Country—also known as *Euskadi*—which lies to the north of Spain in the area surrounding the western part of the Pyrenees. The Basques have a proud and independent streak that goes back to ancient times; and tales abound of the difficulties invaders such as the Romans faced trying to bring them under control. Like other regions in Spain, they have developed their own special customs and traditions, including a penchant for culinary feasts and unusual sports. Amongst the latter is *pelota*, a game that is similar to squash but involves around eight players wearing special gloves. Others include caber-tossing, stone-lifting, and woodcutting. Their language, known in Basque as *Euskera*, whose origin is shrouded in mystery, has created a great deal of interest and is a major component in Basque identity. It is older and quite unrelated to the other major European languages, which trace their roots back to a common linguistic stock. This fact has given rise to interesting, though somewhat fanciful, myths that it was the original language spoken in Europe.

Basque nationalism began to gain ground at the end of the last century. In the mid-1880s, the Basques suffered a blow to their autonomy when they officially lost their traditional system of local administration—a privilege they had had enjoyed for centuries—as a result of increased centralization by the Spanish government. Many Basques deeply resented the interference of the government in Madrid and channelled their dissatisfaction into a growing nationalist movement, which was spearheaded by the Basque Nationalist Party (PNV).

The desire for autonomy led two of the Basque provinces to side with the Republicans during the Civil War, and this contributed to the stormy relationship between the region and Franco's dictatorship. The regime, which was rabidly opposed to the slightest hint of autonomy, set about repressing all forms of nationalist sentiment. In the case of the Basques, this was done in an openly punitive fashion. After all, Franco's Spain was declared one "One, Great and Free!" There was no room for division—the unity of Spain was inviolable. Since political parties were outlawed, the PNV went underground. A Basque government-in-exile was maintained throughout the dictatorship, but its role was little more than symbolic. The Basque language was outlawed, and in an attempt to maintain it, Basque parents sent their children to *toikostolas*, unauthorized schools that taught Euskera. Keeping the language alive became a matter of pride.

## ETA and the Rise of Violence

Disillusioned with the passivity of the PNV, in the 1950s a small group of students set about forming their own political organization, *Euzkadi ta Askatasuna*, meaning "Basque Nation and Liberty," and known to the world as ETA. Breaking away from the moderate line taken by the PNV and the Basque government-in-exile, after various internal disputes ETA emerged as an underground separatist revolutionary organization. In 1967, ETA made the chilling decision to commit itself fully to violence as a means to achieve its goals. Despite the fact that the number of active members of ETA was extremely low, its actions had a profound effect on the Franco regime.

The government and ETA embarked on a "tit-for-tat" campaign, with ETA assassinating military officials and the regime responding by effectively punishing the whole region. One of the regime's weapons was the imposition of the State of Emergency. Perhaps more than anything else, this blanket measure, or reprisal, did more to foster the feeling of unity so often reserved for communities facing a common enemy in times of war. The State of Emergency meant an almost complete suspension of civil rights, leaving suspects at the mercy of aggressive police and army tactics. The measure was declared six times in the Basque provinces between 1960 and 1977. Furthermore, in the lawlessness that often ensued, pro-Franco vigilantes took advantage of the situation to launch attacks on those they considered "undesirables." Spanish jails were filled with a disproportional numbers of Basque political prisoners, and at times the climate in the region was one of fear.

Because of its sheer nerve, ETA became a symbol of resistance throughout the country. What was seen as excessively brutal treatment of ETA suspects united the whole opposition throughout the nation in sympathy. In the Basque region, the distinctions traditionally being made between Basque and Spanish were becoming increasingly hazy, while "Basqueness" was becoming a byword for "suffering" unfairly at the hands of the regime.

## The Last Days of the Dictator

By the early 1970s, things were beginning to look uneasy. In 1973, a world economic crisis brought on by an increase in the price of petrol put an end to the economic "miracle" in Spain. The following year saw a sharp rise in inflation, coupled with increasing working-class agitation. Furthermore, the old dictator was now in his eighties and clearly showing signs of frailty. Since 1939, he had been the ultimate authority in the nation; and it was now becoming abundantly clear that he was not immortal. Although he had named his successor, Juan Carlos, nobody could really imagine what would happen after his death. Amidst the uncertainty, the voice of opposition to the regime was growing—indeed, even the Church found several of its members questioning the dictatorship.

For the first time since coming to power, Franco relaxed his grip on power; he handed the job of running the government to another man. In June 1973, Admiral Luis Carrero Blanco was named prime minister. Franco, still the head of state, had hoped the admiral would get down to the task of ensuring that the regime continue after him with as little fuss as possible. However, in December that same year, Carrero Blanco was assassinated in a daring bomb attack by ETA terrorists. Franco swiftly replaced him with Carlos Arias Navarro, a civilian, who immediately attempted to tackle the growing crisis by announcing a package of reforms aimed at addressing some of the complaints directed at the regime. Yet, few saw this as anything more than a desperate attempt to ensure the survival of the regime. In the meantime, violence was spiraling and the security forces battled harder to suppress displays of

The Valle de los Caídos (Valley of the Fallen), which houses
Franco's tomb. Although intended as a memorial to the dead on
both sides of the Civil War, it was in fact built by Republican
prisoners of war, many of whom suffered extreme hardship
and even death during the course of its construction.
The huge cross is 150m tall and 46m wide.

regional nationalism and to stamp out the terrorists. The more this
went on, the more Franco's dictatorship increasingly lost credibility
amongst the population.

Then in 1975, Franco's health deteriorated sharply and it became
clear that he was nearing the end. For two months, doctors did all they
could to keep the dictator alive. Finally, on November 20, General
Franco was declared dead. Spain now had a new leader, Juan Carlos I.

# A Remarkable Transition to Democracy

"After Franco what?" was the question that was on everyone's lips before the death of the dictator. Few people knew what was in the mind of the man Franco had chosen as his successor. Juan Carlos I had given very little away, and most had taken this to be a sign that he was little more than Franco's own creation, reared on a diet of the dictator's own values and ready to help keep the regime's torch burning. They were wrong. Privately, Juan Carlos had acknowledged the importance of re-establishing democracy in Spain and peacefully laying to rest the long years of dictatorship; and he was to play a crucial role in bringing this about. What few people knew was that for several years Juan Carlos had secretly met with members of the oppostion (in some cases they had to be smuggled into his residence in the trunks of cars), and he was incredibly well-informed of the country's mood.

Yet Juan Carlos had to tread carefully. He had publicly sworn to defend a regime over whose end he was about to preside. In order to dismantle the structures of the dictatorship, the new monarch needed a prime minister who was acceptable to the regime, but who could also initiate a dialogue with the illegal opposition. Arias Navarro would clearly be an obstacle to the process since he owed not only his job but his ideology to Franco. In July 1976, Juan Carlos substituted him with Adolfo Suárez, a man he felt had the skills to do the job. Súarez did not disappoint. From the beginning, the king and Suárez were clear that it would be impossible to bring about the end of the dictatorship by using the same kind of authoritarian means that had been used by Franco. Neither the regime's supporters nor the opposition would allow such a plan to succeed. Therefore, they worked on the principle that the key to a peaceful transition to democracy was to establish a pact with the opposition in order to negotiate a break with the past. Thankfully the opposition was almost unanimous in its agreement to play by the rules of the pact.

Having managed to get the co-operation of the greater part of the opposition, the government announced the Law of Political Reform, which was designed to legalize political parties and introduce the right to vote. This measure was approved by the Cortes in November, and subsequently endorsed by referendum in December. If democracy was to be successful, all of the opposition parties were going to have to be permitted to participate in the elections. But Suárez had to tread carefully when it came to some of the old enemies of the regime. Free elections would involve the participation of the Communists, and this idea was wholly unacceptable to Franco's diehard supporters (who had already had to swallow the bitter pill

Juan Carlos I.

of partial amnesties for ETA terrorists). Yet after negotiations with with Santiago Solares, leader of the Spanish Communist Party, Suárez went ahead and legalized the party in April 1977. In a clear show of compromise, the Communists put aside their Republican ideals and agreed to work within a constitutional monarchy.

Meanwhile tension was growing in the country as ETA stepped up its violent campaign against the government with a spate of assassinations and kidnappings. Other militant extremists from both sides of the political spectrum became increasingly active too, raising the specter of a bloody showdown. Undeterred, the king and Suárez went ahead with the plan. In March, Juan Carlos decreed that the first free general elections would take place on June 15, 1977—the first in Spain since 1936. It was a momentous occasion. Amidst a wave of national euphoria, the elections were celebrated fairly and freely. The electoral turnout was enormous as the people rushed to the polling stations to play their part in the history that was being made. Two parties took the lion's share of the votes, the Democratic Center Union (UCD) with around 36 percent, led by Suárez himself, and the Spanish Socialist Party (PSOE) with 29 percent. Although many had expected the Communist Party to win the contest, it secured only 9 percent of the votes. UCD and PSOE were both moderate parties that together covered a broad area of the political center ground. The result indicated the understandable caution of the nation and allowed Suárez to continue to oversee the reforms of the country.

On October 31, 1978, a new constitution, drawn up with the participation of the opposition, was approved by the Cortes and then endorsed by referendum. This time the politicians were determined not to repeat the same mistakes made in the past. The Church that was once declared to be "inseparable from the national conscience" and the inspiration of its laws was made to feel a welcome part of the democracy. Although the constitution affirmed that there would no longer be a state religion, it promised a future of co-operation with the Catholic Church in a conciliatory tone. This seemingly minor gesture was of great importance, since it helped to alleviate the tensions created previously by the Republican constitution of 1931. The short-lived republic of the 1930s had attempted to deny the Church any participation in the affairs of the State, going so far as to refuse it the right "to exercise industry, commerce, or teaching." It paid a high price for its bluntness.

An area of utmost sensitivity was that concerning the unity of Spain. The very mention of Basque or Catalan independence was enough to jeopardize the whole transitional process—the army simply would not tolerate such talk. Yet the issue could not be ignored. Accordingly, the new constitution affirmed that the unity of the nation was "indissoluble" but it neverthless recognized that the regions were entitled to a degree of autonomy. Such a declaration would have amounted to an act of sedition under Franco who, along with his supporters, had elevated the unity of Spain and its people to an almost mystical level. The regions were soon to exploit the concession to great effect.

The democratic elections and the content of the new constitution marked a major turning point in the history of Spain, demonstrating the success of the process of converting Spain into a democracy after many long years of dictatorship. But a weak point was its failure to address the problems of the Armed Forces—victors of the Civil War, and one of the pillars of Franco's regime. With Franco gone, only Juan Carlos I could expect the loyalty of the army. To reduce the possibility military intervention in the political process, Suárez tactfully appointed a military officer, not a civilian, as Minister of Defense to oversee reforms of the Armed Forces. Lieutenant General Manuel Gutiérrez Mellado, a liberal, began a process of substituting key military officers with others who were more sympathetic to the changes taking place. Gutiérrez was no revolutionary and, in keeping with the spirit of the transition, worked slowly and cautiously. Overall, the process brought beneficial results, helping to neutralize potentially troublesome elements in the army and isolating those that were most reactionary.

However, the intrigues of the ultra-conservative military officers were about to dramatically challenge the fledgling democracy. In August 1978, an ETA faction launched a series of attacks against the armed forces. It was a blatant attempt to sabotage the parliamentary ratification of the constitution and the subsequent referendum. The army was, not surprisingly, incensed by such an act of provocation. In the events that followed, several officers hatched a plan, named Operation Galaxy, to stage a coup. The government was alerted. As a result, two leading conspirators were arrested. One of the officers seized was Antonio Tejero Molina, a lieutenant colonel in the Guardia Civil, the militarized police force. The plan had failed, but the government's timid reaction and the subsequent leniency of the military tribunal was anything but a lesson to deter would-be coup leaders.

Operation Galaxy had never gotten past the planning stage, but the attempted coup of February 23, 1981 did. This time, the very same Tejero and his henchmen stormed into the Cortes, during the investiture of Leopoldo Calvo Sotelo as Spain's new prime minister, and held the assembly at gun-point. The whole democratic process was hanging on a thread. The nation, watching the events as they unfolded live on television, held its breath.

If the goverment lacked influence over the army, could the king persuade it? The authority of Juan Carlos was put to the test. As ministers and parliamentary deputies waited for an end to their ordeal as

Tejero's hostages, the king declared that the Crown did not and would not support any attack against democracy. He personally contacted key senior military officials and, by making his position clear, managed to win their loyalty. Deprived of royal support, the coup failed. The fact that the government owed its survival to the king was proof of the fragility of democracy. Although the king met with the political opposition and informed them that he could not repeat what he had just done, the new democracy had passed the biggest test. It had overcome the army.

## Spain under the Felipe González and the Socialists

That same year saw serious problems hit the government. Súarez had already been replaced by Calvo Sotelo as prime minister. His UCD party was disintegrating, shaken by internal disputes over the direction it was taking, and Suárez had found his position untenable. The government limped on, but many UCD members defected to other newly created parties. Faced with a crisis of confidence, there was little to do but ask the king to dissolve the Cortes, and announce general elections.

On October 28, 1982, the Socialists, headed by Felipe González, an immensely popular and able Andalucían lawyer who had played a key role in the democratic negotiations after Franco's death, won a sweeping victory in the general elections. UCD gained only 6.5 percent of the votes compared to PSOE's 48 percent. This margin was highly significant. It was now clear that, having elected a Socialist government into power, the Spanish people were determining their own future. The various elements that continued to have an interest in destabilizing democracy, although they did not disappear, were becoming more isolated and discredited. The transition had succeeded. The governing of the country had passed on to the opposition by peaceful and democratic means—a great achievement that owed it success to the moderation and co-operation shown by practically all sides.

From November 1982 to March 1996, Spain was governed by the Socialist government led by Felipe González. It was a period of enormous socio-economic change as the country fully embraced the

modern world. Despite its name, the
Socialist Party to which González
belonged had little to do with Marxist
ideology, which it had renounced several
years earlier. It was a highly dynamic party
that attracted a wide range of supporters
from not only the left but also the center.
Although moderate in tone, the Socialists
demonstrated a tough and active style of
government that oversaw major reforms in
a variety of areas including education,
welfare, industry, and taxation. It also
launched into much-needed programs
to develop the infrastructure of the

Felipe González.

country, overseeing the construction of much needed major roads.

Yet there was one prize the government anxiously pursued—entry
into that powerful economic club, the European Community (now the
European Union). For a long time, many politicians from both the left
and right had dreamed of such a day; and on January 1, 1986, it arrived,
bringing to a successful conclusion several years of hard work and
negotiations. Also that same year, after putting the issue to the nation in
a referendum, Spain's full incorporation into NATO was approved.

The country enjoyed stability and peace under the Socialists, and the
government continued to enjoy huge popular support. Of course, it was
not a problem-free ride. The government was unable to bring down the
high level of unemployment. By the end of the 1980s, the number of
jobless was running at over 20 percent, making it one of the worst hit
countries in Europe, and causing a great deal of social hardship.
Another seemingly insoluble problem was the terrorist group ETA, a
law unto itself, which continued to wage a violent campaign to bring
about Basque independence.

Felipe González and PSOE held on to power after a succession of
general election victories—four in total. But by the early 1990s, the
administration was running into trouble. The economy was seriously

José María Aznar.

affected by a world recession. Furthermore, a series of scandals involving corruption rocked the government. Meanwhile, one of the opposition parties, the conservative People's Party (PP) was growing stronger and stronger. Despite one more final victory in the elections of 1993, PSOE was increasingly beleaguered and on the defensive as yet more scandals emerged. In March 1996, after an extraordinary lengthy tenure in government, Felipe González and his party lost the elections to the Partido Popular. Spain had a new prime minister, José María Aznar. The pendulum had swung once again, and it had done so once more without blood.

## Spain in the 21st Century

The days of Franco are gone and the future for Spain looks secure. After many years of isolation, Spain has embraced democracy and opened its doors wide open to the new political and economic spirit of the European Union. Aznar's government faced many challenges as the 20th century drew to a close, yet Spain enjoyed a period of economic prosperity and mercifully saw some progress in reducing the number of the unemployed. With the inevitable replacement of the peseta by the European single currency, the euro, Spain has shown the world clearly that its future lies in Europe.

One of the greatest challenges facing the Spanish government as the new millennium dawned was the seemingly intractable problem of terrorism in the Basque Country. Sadly, attempts to negotiate an end to the hostilities by ETA continued to end in failure. The organization continued its violent and bloody campaign in the name of Basque independence, despite the clear message from the overwhelming majority of Basques, and the Spanish population at large, that enough was enough.

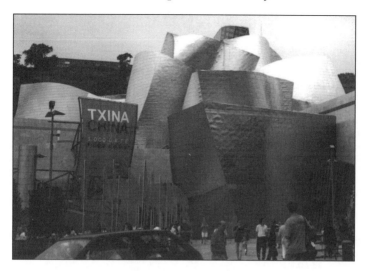

The modern face of Spain—the Guggenheim Museum of Modern Art
in the the Basque city of Bilbao.

Nevertheless, Spain enjoys a reputation as a safe and vibrant country
to live in and visit, and this ensures that it remains one of the most
popular destinations for travelers in Europe. Of course, as we have seen,
Spain's history encompasses not only its geographical boundaries, but is
inextricably linked to the pasts of Europe, Africa, the Middle East,
South America, the USA, and even South-East Asia. As a result, it has
proved to be a fascinating example of how different peoples of the world
have interacted with each other, shaping each others' identities and destinies.
Despite the upheavals of its past and previous attempts to impose
regional unity by force, Spain has paraxodically blossomed into a country
united by its diversity, which it proudly displays for all to see.

As the world today grows ever smaller, particularly in a Western
Europe that has embraced full political and economic unity, it is a cause
for celebration to see that differences continue to thrive, making the
world all the richer for it.

# INDEX

Abd al-Malik, son of Al-Mansur, 40
Abd al-Rahman, 30
Abd al-Rahman II, 31
Abd al-Rahman III, 31
Abd-el-Krim, Muhammad, 127, 128, 129
Adrian of Utrecht, 72
Alans, 22
Alba, Duke of, 77
Alcalá Zamora, Niceto, 135
Alfonso V of Portugal, 59
Alfonso VI, 46, 47
Alfonso XI of Castilla, 50, 53
Alfonso XII, 114, 117, 123
Alfonso XIII, 117, 123-124, 128, 130-131, 139, 152
Al-Hakem II, 35, 38
Alhambra, Granada, 10
Al-Mansur, 38-40, 46, 50
Almohad Berbers, 48, 63
Almoravids, 46
Amadeo I, 112-113
Americas: discovery and colonization by Spain, 68-71; exploitation of gold and silver by Spanish Crown, 70; Independence from Spain, 103-105; representation in the Cádiz Constitution of 1812, 101
Anarchism, see CNT
Andalucía, 12, 15, 86, 146
Anjou, Duke of, see Felipe V
Anti-Semitism, 63; during Inquisition 65-67; in Visigoth Kingdom 24
Aragón, 40, 45, 48, 49, 50, 53, 56, 57, 58, 71, 73, 86, 89, 90, 107, 131; territorial expansion during reconquest, 48-50
Aranjuez, 98
Arias Navarro, Carlos, 160, 162
Arte Nouveau, 120
Assyrians, 15
Asturias, 36, 38, 50, 137

Ayamonte, Marquis of, 86
Azaña, Manuel, 132, 133, 135, 139
Aztecs, 70

Badajoz, 45, 46
Balearic Islands, 48
Barcelona, 39, 40, 86, 111, 120, 124, 142
Basque country, 7, 90, 107, 136, 158-159, 164, 167
Basque language, origins, 158
Basque Nationalist Party, see PNV
Bebb, Captain Cecil, 139, 140
Berber invasion of Spain, 27
Berbers, 10, 28, 30, 39, 40, 48, 63
Berenguer, Dámaso, 130, 131
Black Death, 50
Bloque Nacional (National Bloc), 138, 139
Bolivar, Simón de Bolivar, 104
Bourbon dynasty: new royal house of Spain, 89; deposed in revolution of 1868, 112; restoration after War of Independence, 102-103; restoration in 1876, 114, 115
Braque, Georges, 148
Britain, 96, 100, 142
British Royal Air Force, 139

Caciquismo, 116, 124
Cádiz 15, 96, 100, 105
Caliphate of Córdoba, 31-36; fall of, 40-41
Calvo Sotelo, José, 139
Calvo Sotelo, Leopoldo, 165
Cambó, Francesc, 126
Canadiense, strike in Barcelona, 127
Canary Islands, 139
Cánovas del Castillo, Antonio, 115-118, 123, 138
Cantabrians, 23
Cape St. Vincente, Battle of, 96

# Index

Carrrero Blanco, Luis Admiral, 160
Carlist Party, 113, 114, 138, 139, 140, 141
Carlist Wars, 107-109
Carlos II, 87, 89
Carlos III, 91-94, 95, 98
Carlos IV, 94-98
Carlos I of Spain (Carlos V, Holy Roman Emperor), 71-74, 76, 77, 90
Carlos VI, 98
Carlos, brother of Fernando VII and rival to the Spanish throne, 107
Carmelites, 74-76
Carthage, 17
Castilla, 38, 40, 45, 48-50, 53, 54, 55, 56, 57, 59, 60, 65, 71, 72, 73, 86, 89, 90, 140
Castilla-León, territorial expansion during reconquest, 48-50
Catalan counties, 45
Catalan nationalism 130
Catalonia, 57, 107, 111, 113, 120, 127, 144, 150; rebellion against the Spanish Crown in 1640, 86; rebellion against central government in 1917, 126; autonomy during the Second Spanish Republic, 136-137,
Catholic Monarchs, see Isabella I and Fernando II of Aragón
CEDA (Confederación Española de Derechas Autonomas), 135-138
Celtiberians, 15-17
Celts, 15-17
Cervantes, 85
Cervantes, Miguel de, 84-85
Ceuta, 12
Charlemagne, 72
Charles Dickens, 132
Charles, Archduke of Austria, 89, 90
Church: liberal attack on Church lands in 1830s, 108; reforms during the Second Spanish Republic, 133, 134; special status in Franco regime, 151; treatment in 1978 constitution, 164
Civil War, 5, 137, 148, 149, 151, 157, 165
Climate, 12

CNT (National Confederation of Workers,) 125, 126, 134, 135, 137, 138
Colombia, Independence, 104
Columbus, Christopher, 12, 68
Comisiones Obreras (Workers' Commissions), 157
Communism, 144, 149, 154, 157, 163
Communist Party, 163, 164
Companys, Lluis, 137
Condor Legion, bombing of Spain, 142
Conquistadors, 12, 70
Constitution: 1812 Cádiz, 100-103, 104, 105; during regency of María Christina, 108; during reign of Isabel II, 110; after liberal revolution of 1869, 112; of 1876, 115, 139
Conversos, 65
Córdoba, 30, 49, 142; see also Caliphate of Córdoba
Corsica, 17
Cortés, Hernán, 70
Council of Blood, 77
Council of Castilla, 90
Covadonga, 38
Covadonga, Battle of, 36
Cristina of Hapsburg, María, 117
Cristina, María, regent of Spain and mother of Isabel, II 107
Cuba, 8, 105, 113; independence from Spain, 118-120
Cubism, 148

Dalí, Salvador, 146, 148-151
Dato, Eduardo, 126, 127
Discalced (Barefoot) Carmelites, 75
Don Quixote, 84
Doña Perfecta, novel by Galdós, 114
Drake, Sir Francis, 78

Egmont, Count, 77
El Cid, 46-47
"El Desastre," the loss of Cuba 119
El Escorial, 81, 82
El Greco, 81-82, 87
Elisabeth Farnese of Parma, 91

Elizabeth I of England, 78
Emigration of Spanish workers to
    Western Europe during Franco
    regime, 156-157
Emirate of al-Andalus, 30
Emperor Leopold I, 89
Enlightenment, 93
Enrique II de Trastámara, 53
Enrique IV of Castilla, 57-58
Espartero, General Baldomero, 108-109,
    111
Esquilache, Marquis of, 92
ETA, 7, 159-160, 163, 165, 167
European Union, 7, 167, 168
*Euskadi*, see Basque country
*Euskera, see* Basque Language
*Exaltados,* 105, 106, 108

Falange Española Tradicionalista y de
    las JONS, 141
Falange Party, 138, 139
Felipe I, 78
Felipe II, 74, 76-81
Felipe III, 82-84, 85
Felipe IV, 85-87: Patron of Velázquez,
    87-88
Felipe V, 89-90
Fernández, Giménez 137
Fernando I of Castilla-León, 45, 46
Fernando II (*El Católico*) of Aragón, 45,
    56, 57-62, 67, 71
Fernando III of Castilla-León 48-49, 50
Fernando VI, 91-92
Fernando VII, 97, 98, 99, 102, 103, 104,
    106, 107
Ferrer y Guardia, Francisco, 124
Feudalism, 24, 108
Floridablanca, Count of, 93, 95
France, 53, 73, 87, 95, 98, 100, 106,
Francis I of France, 72
Francis I, king of France, 73
Franco, 5, 12, 137, 149, 162, 164, 168;
    role in Civil War, 139-146;
    Dictatorship, 151-161
Franks, 23

French, Revolution 94
Frente, Popular (Popular Front) 138
*Fueros,* 90

Galdós, Benito Pérez, 114
Galicia, 50, 140
García Lorca, Federico, 146-148
Gaudí, Antoni, 120-123
Geography of Spain, 12
Germany, 146
Gibraltar, 10, 27, 28, 90, 140
Gil Robles, José María 135, 138
Godoy, Manuel, 95, 96, 98
González, Felipe, 166-168
Goths, 23
Goya, Francisco, 99
Granada, 10, 38, 41, 45, 46, 50, 57,
    146, 147; capitulation of, 60-62
Greeks, 15
Gregory IX, Pope, 65
Guadelete, Battle of, 27, 38
Güell, Count Eusebi, 120
Guernica, destruction during Civil War,
    144, 149
*Guernica,* painting by Picasso, 144,
    149
Gutiérrez Mellado, Manuel, 165
Gypsy folklore in García Lorca's work,
    146, 147

Hannibal, 17
Hapsburgs, 71-74, 76, 89
Havana, 119
Hawkins, John, 78
Henry VIII of England, 72
*Hermandades,* 55, 56
Hidalgo, Miguel, 104
Híjar, Duke of, 86
Hisham II, 38
Hitler, Adolf, 135, 142, 144
Holland, Independence from Spain, 87
Hornes, Count, 77

Iberians, 15-17
Incas, 70

Innocent X, Pope, 88
International Brigades, 142
Isabel II, 107-112, 113
Isabel of Portugal, Princess, 80
Isabella I (*La Católica*) of Castilla, 45, 56, 57-62, 71; creation of Spanish Inquisition, 62-67
Islamic Spain, 10, 27-31, 38-41, 83
Italy, 57, 73, 91, ; loss of Italian possessions by the Spanish Crown in 1713, 87

Jaime I of Aragón, 48
Japan, 156
Jesuits, 76, 93, 134
Jews, 29, 35, 63; expulsion from Spain, 67; *see also* Anti-Semitism
John of the Cross, St., *see* Juan de la Cruz
José I (Joseph Bonaparte), 98-99, 102, 103
Juan Carlos I of Spain, 7, 152-3, 161, 162-163, 165-166
Juan de Bourbon, 152-153
Juan de la Cruz, San (St. John of the Cross), 74, 75
Juan IV, 87
Juana, daughter of Enrique IV, 58, 59, 60
Juana, Queen, 71, 72
Junta Central Suprema, 100-101
Juntas Militares, military unions, 125-6

La Barraca (*The Barrack*), García Lorca's theatre troupe, 147
Labor organizations under Franco,
Land: inheritance laws, 55; reform in the 1830s, 108; reform during Second Spanish Republic, 133
Language: in Roman Spain, 18; present-day, 7
Largo Caballero, Francisco, 137, 138, 144
Las Meninas (Maids of Honor), painting by Velázquez, 88

Las Navas de Tolosa, Battle of, 48
Latin language, 18
Latin America, *see* Americas
León, 39, 40, 45, 50, 140
Leonor de Guzmán, 53
Leovigild, Visigothic king, 23, 24
Lerma, Duke of, 84
Lerroux, Alejandro, 135
Liberalism, 100-103, 105-107, 110, 114, 116
Lorca, *see* García Lorca
Louis XIV of France, 89
Louis XVI of France, 95

Madrid, 92, 105, 106, 108, 111, 112, 146; resists Nationalist attacks in Civil War, 142; riots during reign of Carlos III, 92
Maine, US battleship, 119
Málaga, 15, 148
Mallorca, 73
Margarita, princess, 88
Marie Antoinette, 95
Marshall Plan, 154
Martínez de la Rosa, Francisco, 108
Maura, Antonio, 124
Maximilian, Holy Roman Emperor, 71, 72
Maya, 70
Medina-Sidonia, Duke of, 86
Melilla, 12, 140
Mendizábal, Juan Álvarez, 108
Mexico City, 70
Mexico, independence from Spain, 104
Michelangelo, 81
Milan, 87
Military revolt: in 1850s, 111; in 1868, 112; in 1874, 113; in Spanish Morocco, in 1936 140
Minorca, 49
Miranda, Francisco de, 104
Miró, Joan, 150
Moderados, 105, 108, 110
Mola, General, 139
Moor, explanation of term, 30
*Moriscos*, 67; expulsion from Spain by Felipe III, 83

Moroccan crisis, 127, 129
Morocco, 12, 111, 140
Mosque of Córdoba, 10, 11, 33, 50
Movimiento Nacional, 151
*Mozárabes*, 29
Muhammad II, 40
Muhammad, Prophet, 28
Mühlberg, Battle of (painting of Carlos
    V by Titian), 81
Mussolini, Benito, 141, 144

Naples, 57, 87, 92
Napoleon Bonaparte, 96-102, 103
Napoleonic Wars, 96-98
Narváez, Ramón María, 110
National Institute of Industry,
Navarra, 45, 48, 50, 57, 90, 107, 113,
    138
NATO, 167
Negrín, Juan, 144
Nelson, Lord Horatio, 96
Netherlands, 77
Nobility, 53-56

October Revolution, revolt in Asturia
    and Catalonia, 137
Olivares, Count Duke, of 85-7, 90
Opus Dei, 155
Organización Sindical,
Ortega y Gasset, José, 120
Ottoman Empire, 73, 85

Pacto del Pardo, 117
Pamplona, 39
Parc Güell, 121
Partido Radical, 135
Pedro I, "el Cruel", 53
Pelayo, Visigothic king, 38
Peru, 70
Peseta, first introduction, 111
Philippines, 8, 118, 119
Phonoecians, 15
Picasso, Pablo, 144, 148-151
Pizarro, Francisco, 70
Plague, 50, 83

PNV (Basque Nationalist Party), 158,
    159
Political sytem, present, 7
Portugal, 12, 50, 57, 59, 60, 96, 97, 98;
    annexed by Spain in 1580, 80;
    independence from Spain, 87
PP (People's Party), 167-168
Prado Museum, 88, 93, 99, 149
Prieto, Indalecio, 138
Prim y Prats, Juan, 112, 113
Primo de Rivera, 128-9, 139
Primo de Rivera, José Antonio, 141, 142
*Pronuciamientos*, 11-13, 115, 131, 139-40
Protestant problem: during Carlos V's
    reign, 73; during Felipe II's reign, 77
PSOE (Spanish Socialist Party), 164,
    166-168
Puerto Rico, 105, 118, 119

Reconquest of Spain, 45-54; origins,
    36-38; completion in 1492, 62-62
Reccared, Visigothic king, 24
Religion: in Muslim Spain, 29; in Roman
    Spain, 20
Republic, Second: first administration
    under Socialists, 131-135; second
    administration under influence of
    right, 135-139; under Socialists
    during Civil War, 139-146
Republicans, 113, 126, 132, 133, 134,
    136, 142, 144; *see also* Republic,
    Second
Revolution: in Cuba, 118; liberal
    revolution of 1868, 112-113
*Reyes Católicos, see* Isabella I and
    Fernando II of Aragón
Robles, Gil, 138
Rodrigo Díaz de Vivar, see *El Cid*
Rodrigo, Visigothic king, 25, 27
Roman Empire, 10, 17-21; early
    conquest of Spain, 10, 17-18, 81

Sagasta, Práxedes Mateo, 117
Sagrada Familia, Barcelona, 122
Saint Ignatious Loyola, 93

# Index

Salamanca, 76, 140
Santiago, 50
Santiago de Compostela, 39, 72
Santo Domingo, Caribbean island, 95
Sardinia, 17, 87
Sebastian, king of Portugal, 80
Seigneurialism, 72
*Semana Trágica*, 124
Señoríos, land inheritance, 55
Serrano, Francisco, 112
Sevilla, 45, 46, 50, 71, 83, 100, 142
Sicily, 17, 57, 87
Slavery in Cuba, 118
Socialists, 124, 126, 127, 131, 132, 133, 134, 137; *see also* PSOE
Solares, Santiago, 163
Spanish Armada, 77, 78
Spanish Inquisition, 62, 67, 68
Spanish, language, 8
Suárez, Adolfo, 162, 165
Suebi, 22
Sulayman, 40
Surrealism, 147

*Taifas*, 41-43, 46, 47, 48
Tarifa, 10
Tariq ibn Ziyad, General (leader of Arab invasion of Spain), 27
Teatre-Museu Dalí, Figueres, 151
Tejero Molina, Antonio, 165-166
Telegraph, first introduction, 111
Teresa de Jesús, Santa (St. Teresa of Ávila), 74-76
Tetuán, 111
Thirty Years War, 85
Titian, 81
Toledo, 45, 47, 75, 82; seized from Muslims by Alfonso VI, 46
Topete, Juan, 112
Toro, Battle of, 59
Torquemada, Tomás de, (Grand Inquistitor), 67
Trafalgar, Battle of, 96, 101

Trastámara dynasty, 53
Tribute payment, 45
*Turno pacífico*, system of alternating governements created by Cánovas, 115-118

UCD (Demorcratic Center Union), 163, 164-166
UGT, General Union of Workers, 125, 126, 130, 137
Umayyads, 27-31
Unamuno, Miguel de, 120
Unión de Armas (Union of Arms), 86
Unión Militar Española, 139
United Nations, 155
United States, 5, 8, 102, 142, 147, 155; role in loss of Cuba, 118
Utrecht, Treaty of, 89

Valencia, 47, 49, 57, 73, 83
Vandals, 22
Vatican, 65
Velázquez, Diego, 87
Venezuela, 104
Vienna, 73
Vietnam, 111
Villalar, Battle of, 73
Visigoths, 10, 23-5, 29, 36, 38; conquest of Spain, 22; fall of Visigothic kingdom, 27
Voltaire, 132

Wall Street Crash, 130
Wamba, Visigothic king, 24
War of Independence, 98-102
War of the Spanish Succession, 89-90
Wellington, Duke of, 102
Workers Unions, 125, 16; *see also* CNT, Comisiones Obreras, and Juntas Militares
World War I, 125
World War II, 144